SINGLES
THE SECRET BEHIND THE SMILE

General Editor
LYMAN COLEMAN

Managing Editor
DENISE BELTZNER

Assistant Editors
DOUGLAS LABUDDE
KEITH MADSEN

Cover Art
CHRISTOPHER WERNER

Cover Design
ERICA TIEPEL

Layout Production
FRONTLINE GROUP

Reference Notes by Richard Peace, ©1984, 1985, 1986, Serendipity House.

Seven Issues Vital to Singles

Session		Track One	Track Two
1	ORIENTATION	Finding Community: Acts 2:42–47	
2	MY STORY	Leaving Home: Lk. 15:11–32	My Strengths & Stresses: 2 Co. 11:21–31
3	CHOICES	A World of Choices: Mk. 1:9–20	The Single Advantage: 1 Co. 7:8–9, 25–35
4	SEXUALITY	A Touching Act: Lk. 7:36–50	Learning Control: 1 Thes. 4:1–8
5	REJECTION	You Can't Go Home Again: Lk. 4:14–30	Rejected by Men: 1 Pe. 2:4–10
6	LONELINESS	Loneliness vs. Aloneness: Mt. 26:36–46	Oh, Lonesome Me: 2 Ti. 4:9–22
7	TOMORROW	Stay Tuned: Jn. 16:5–13	Stay Loose: Phil. 4:10–13

Serendipity / Box 1012 / Littleton, CO 80160   (800)525-9563

Beginning a Small Group

1. PURPOSE: This course is designed for 101 groups to continue. The goal is to get better acquainted and become a support group. We call this the "formation period" of a group or 201. Using the analogy of a baseball diamond, the goal is home plate or "bonding." To get to home plate, the group needs to go around 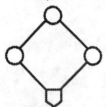 three bases: FIRST BASE: History Giving—telling your "story" to one another—your childhood, your journey, your hopes and dreams. SECOND BASE: Affirmation—responding to each other's story with appreciation. THIRD BASE: Need Sharing—going deeper in your story—your present struggles, roadblocks, anxieties, and where you need help from God and the group.

2. AGENDA: There are three parts to every group meeting:

GATHERING / 10 min.	BIBLE STUDY / 30 min.	CARING / 20 min.
Purpose: To break the ice and become better acquainted	Purpose: To share your spiritual journey	Purpose: To share prayer requests and pray

3. FEARLESS FOURSOME: If you have more than 7 in your group at any time, call the option play when the time comes for Bible study, and subdivide into groups of 4 for greater participation. (In 4's, everyone will share and you can finish the Bible study in 30 minutes.) Then regather the group for the Caring Time.

GATHERING	BIBLE STUDY	CARING
All Together	Groups of 4	Back Together

4. EMPTY CHAIR: Pull up an empty chair during the **Caring Time** at the close and ask God to fill this chair each week. Remember, by breaking into groups of four for the Bible study time, you can grow numerically without feeling "too big" as a group.

The Group Leader needs an Apprentice in training at all times so that the Apprentice can start a new "cell" when the group size is twelve or more.

INSTRUCTIONS FOR GROUP LEADER

PURPOSE: **What is this course all about?** To offer singles an opportunity to discuss common issues in their lives in a supportive group relationship.

SEEKERS/ STRUGGLERS: **Who is this course designed for?** Two kinds of people: (a) Seekers who do not know where they are with God but are open to finding out, and (b) Strugglers who are committed to Jesus Christ, but want to grow in their faith.

NEW PEOPLE: **Does this mean I can invite my non-church friends?** Absolutely. In fact, this would be a good place for people on their way back to God to start.

STUDY: **What are we going to study?** Seven issues vital to singles (see title page) and what the Bible has to say about them. The rest of the agenda is outlined on page 2.

FIRST SESSION: **What do we do at the meetings?** In the first session, you get acquainted and decide on the Ground Rules for your group. In sessions two through seven, you have the option of two Tracks for Bible study.

TWO TRACKS: **What are the two tracks?** TRACK ONE—This study is best for newly-formed groups or groups that are unfamiliar with small group Bible study. This option primarily contains multiple-choice questions, with no "right or wrong" answers.

TRACK TWO—This study is best for groups who have had previous small group Bible studies and want to dig deeper into the Scriptures. The questions are deeper—and the Scripture is a teaching passage.

CHOOSING A TRACK: **Which track of Bible study do you recommend?** The TRACK ONE study is best for newly-formed groups, groups that are unfamiliar with small group Bible study, or groups that are only meeting for an hour. The TRACK TWO study is best for deeper Bible study groups, or groups which meet for more than an hour.

CHOOSING BOTH TRACKS: **Can we choose both tracks?** If your group meets for 90 to 120 minutes, you can choose to do both studies at the same time. Or you can spend two weeks on a unit—TRACK ONE the first week and TRACK TWO the next. Or you can do one of the tracks in the meeting and the other track for homework.

SMALL GROUP: **What is different about this course?** It is written for a small group to do together.

GROUP BUILDING: **What is the purpose behind your approach to Bible study?** To give everyone a chance to share their own "spiritual story," and to bond as a group. This is often referred to as "koinonia."

KOINONIA: What is koinonia and why is it a part of these studies? Koinonia means "fellowship." It is an important part of these sessions, because as a group gets to know one another, they are more willing to share their needs and care for one another.

BIBLE KNOWLEDGE: What if I don't know much about the Bible? No problem. Track One is based on a Bible story that stands on its own—to discuss as though you were hearing it for the first time. Plus there are a few Reference Notes to point out important details. Track Two comes with Comments and complete Reference Notes—to keep you up to speed.

COMMENTS & REFERENCE NOTES: What is the purpose of the Comments and Reference Notes in the studies? To help you understand the context of the Bible passage and any difficult words that need to be defined.

LEADERSHIP: Who leads the meetings? Ideally, there should be three people: (a) trained leader, (b) apprentice or co-leader, and (c) host. Having an apprentice-in-training in the group, you have a built-in system for multiplying the group if it gets too large. In fact, this is one of the goals of the group—to give "birth" to a new group in time.

RULES: What are the ground rules for the group?

Priority: While you are in the course, you give the group meetings priority.

Participation: Everyone participates and no one dominates.

Respect: Everyone is given the right to their own opinion, and "dumb questions" are encouraged and respected.

Confidentiality: Anything that is said in the meeting is never repeated outside the meeting.

Empty Chair: The group stays open to new people at every meeting as long as they understand the ground rules.

Support: Permission is given to call upon each other in time of need at any time.

Continuing: What happens to the group after finishing this course? The group is free to disband or continue to another course. (See pages 62–63 for making a Covenant and continuing together as a group.)

SESSION 1

Orientation

PURPOSE: To get acquainted, to share your expectations, and to decide on the ground rules for your group.

AGENDA: Gathering 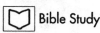 Bible Study ♡ Caring Time

GATHERING / 10 Minutes / All Together

Leader: The purpose of the Gathering Time is to break the ice. Read the instructions for Step One and go first. Then read the Introduction (Step Two) and the instructions for the Bible study. If you are not familiar with the Scripture, read the Reference Notes at the close of the session.

OPEN

Step One: A DAY IN THE LIFE OF YOURS TRULY. Introduce yourself to the group by completing the sentences below. (If there are people in the group who do not know each other, start by having each person give their name.)

1. I usually wake up around...
2. I start the day by...
3. For breakfast I usually eat...
4. My most creative time of the day is...
5. I really get excited about...
6. When I feel "low," I...
7. I enjoy reading...
8. The people I enjoy being around are...
9. My favorite pastime is...
10. I usually get to bed around...

INTRODUCTION

Step Two: Welcome. Welcome to the wonderful world of singleness. Even though many of us choose to be single, it doesn't mean that it's always smooth sailing. Loneliness, sexual tensions, feelings of rejection and problems with friendships are problems that are frequently reported by singles. This course will help us deal with some of these vital issues which affect single adults today.

In this course we will study these issues by following the lives of two single adults—Jesus (Track One studies) and the Apostle Paul (Track Two studies). Through their words and teachings we will consider what the Bible says about friendship, choices, and sexuality. We will then look at what Scripture says concerning rejection and loneliness. Finally, we will consider the future in light of biblical promises.

Being single in today's society is not always easy. It appears that much of society is couple-oriented. But this is changing. The business community was the first to recognize that 21 million Americans live alone. Single-person households have changed the appearance of many things—from the frozen food section of supermarkets to the design of cars rolling off the assembly lines. In addition to the singles who live alone, there are an estimated 58 million singles (who are unmarried, separated, widowed, or divorced) who do not live by themselves.

There are a variety of reasons why so many of us choose the single life. Of course, some of us are single by virtue of divorce or circumstances we didn't always choose: a spouse dies or decides for divorce. Here are some samples:

- Michael (a 35-year-old from Chicago): "If I were married, I wouldn't be as free to make moves on the job as I am now. I am not going to get off track to pick a wife who's not on the same track."
- Donley (a sales representative from the Midwest): "I think marriage is a very serious responsibility and I don't know if I am ready to make that type of commitment."
- Lori (a clerk living on the West Coast): "Once you are single for a while, you get independent and set in your ways. It's hard to let go of that for someone else."
- Leslie (a 42-year-old divorced lawyer): "I never expected to be in this position. My spouse's decision to leave caught me by surprise."

Many of the most important people in the Bible also chose to be single adults. Jeremiah was commanded by God not to marry. John the Baptist and Barnabas were single. The Apostle Paul was single (and possibly a widower). Mary, Martha, and their brother Lazarus were single. And, of course, Jesus himself was single.

Three parts to a session

Every session has three parts: (1) **Gathering**—to break the ice and introduce the topic, (2) **Bible study**—to share your own story through a passage of Scripture, and (3) **Caring**—to decide what action you need to take in this area of your life and to support one another in this action.

In this course, the Bible study approach is a little unique with a different focus. Usually, the focus of the Bible study is the content of the passage. In this course, the focus will be on telling your "story," using the passage as a springboard.

BIBLE STUDY / 30 Minutes / Groups of 4

Leader: If you have more than 7 in this session, we recommend groups of four—4 to sit around the dining table, 4 around the kitchen table, and 4 around a folding table. Ask one person in each foursome to be the Convener and complete the Bible study in the time allowed. Then regather for the Caring Time, allowing 20 minutes.

STUDY | In each foursome ask someone to be the Convener. Read Acts 2:42–47. This passage is a classic description of the supportive fellowship the disciples were able to develop in the early church. Go around on the first question. Then go around with the next question working through the questionnaire. After 30 minutes the Leader will call time and ask you to regather for the Caring Time.

42 They devoted themselves to the apostles' teaching and to the fellowship, to the breaking of bread and to prayer. 43 Everyone was filled with awe, and many wonders and miraculous signs were done by the apostles. 44 All the believers were together and had everything in common. 45 Selling their possessions and goods, they gave to anyone as he had need. 46 Every day they continued to meet together in the temple courts. They broke bread in their homes and ate together with glad and sincere hearts, 47 praising God and enjoying the favor of all the people. And the Lord added to their number daily those who were being saved.

Acts 2:42–47, NIV

1. Had you been alive at the time of these events and been invited to be part of this community, what would have been your initial reaction?
   ❑ sounds too much like socialism to me!
   ❑ I have some things I wouldn't sell for anyone!
   ❑ I might try it for awhile
   ❑ sounds like heaven—where do I sign up?!

2. What possession do you have that you would be very reluctant to sell (Don't worry, we won't ask you to!)?

3. Rate the following elements which were present in the church of Acts in regard to how essential they are to a close fellowship (with 1= most important and 7= least important):
   ___ devotion to teaching that unifies you (v. 42)
   ___ sharing meals (vv. 42, 46)
   ___ sharing in prayer for each other (v. 42)
   ___ sharing exciting and wondrous experiences together (v. 43)
   ___ spending a lot of time together (vv. 44, 46)
   ___ sharing in response to each other's need (vv. 44–45)
   ___ sharing in praise to God (v. 47)

4. When have you come close to sharing in a fellowship experience like the one described here in Acts?
   ❑ in a sorority or fraternity in college
   ❑ in a therapy group
   ❑ in the cast of a play
   ❑ at a job where I worked
   ❑ with some friends in high school
   ❑ in a church-related group
   ❑ working on a political campaign
   ❑ at a bar (like "Cheers")
   ❑ other: _____
   ❑ I've never had this experience

5. Many people's needs in the church of Acts were physical needs that required the sharing of material resources. In your opinion, what are the most important needs of today's singles? (Choose the top two.)
   - ❑ being affirmed as persons of worth
   - ❑ dealing with loneliness
   - ❑ sexual fulfillment
   - ❑ finding support for life stresses
   - ❑ finances
   - ❑ single parenting
   - ❑ having someone to talk to about decisions that need to be made
   - ❑ getting burned in relationships
   - ❑ other: _____

6. What are the most important resources singles need to share in response to those needs? (Again, choose two.)
   - ❑ listening
   - ❑ faith
   - ❑ moral support
   - ❑ mutual affirmation
   - ❑ learning experiences
   - ❑ time (to be with each other)
   - ❑ financial resources
   - ❑ biblical insights
   - ❑ mutual accountability
   - ❑ a networking of resources

7. Which of the resources above do you believe you are best at sharing?

8. What one thing might prevent this group from being a place where you could experience the kind of fellowship described in Acts?
   - ❑ abused trust
   - ❑ phoniness
   - ❑ boring Bible studies
   - ❑ people who dominate the sharing
   - ❑ too much secular input, too little Bible
   - ❑ hypocrisy
   - ❑ my own refusal to risk
   - ❑ people being too "religious"
   - ❑ people refusing to share
   - ❑ too much "baggage"
   - ❑ other: _____

CARING TIME / 20 Minutes / All Together

Leader: In this first session, take some time to discuss your expectations and to decide on the Ground Rules for your group. Then spend the remaining time in caring support for each other through Sharing and Prayer.

1. What motivated you to come to this group?
   - ❑ curiosity
   - ❑ a friend asked me
   - ❑ I had nothing better to do.
   - ❑ a nagging suspicion that I better get my life together

"One of the greatest necessities in America is to discover creative solitude."
—Carl Sandburg

EXPECTATIONS

2. As you begin this group, what are some goals or expectations you have for this course? Choose two or three of the following list and add one of your own:

☐ to get to know some people who are willing to be open and honest about their struggles with being single

☐ to relax and have fun—and forget my singleness for awhile

☐ to see what the Bible has to say about singleness, and the strategies for coping with being single

☐ to deal with some of the issues in my life as a single adult

☐ to see if God is saying anything to me about my life and his will for my life

☐ to learn about the single life by sharing with others

☐ to share my story as a single with others in my group

☐ other: _____

GROUND RULES

3. If you are going to commit the next six weeks or sessions to this group, what are some things you want understood by the group before you commit? Check two or three, and add any of your own:

☐ **Attendance**: to take the group seriously, and to give the meetings priority.

☐ **Confidentiality**: anything that is said in the meetings will not be repeated outside the group.

☐ **Accountability**: the group has the right to hold any member accountable for goals that member sets for himself/herself.

☐ **Responsibility**: every group member accepts responsibility for the care and encouragement of the other group members.

☐ **Openness**: the group is open to any person that is willing to accept the ground rules.

☐ **Duration**: the group will commit to six more sessions. After this, the group will evaluate and recommit to another period if they wish to do so.

SHARING

Take a few minutes to share prayer requests with other group members. Go around and answer this question first:

"How can we help you in prayer this week?"

PRAYER

Take a moment to pray together. If you have not prayed out loud before, finish the sentence:

"Hello, God, this is... (first name). I want to thank you for..."

ACTION

1. Pass around your books and have everyone sign the GROUP DIRECTORY inside the front cover.

2. Ask someone to bring refreshments next week.

3. Encourage the group to invite a friend to the group next week—to fill the "empty chair" (see page 2).

Summary... These disciples (who were part of the church right after it was born at Pentecost) experienced an intensely close fellowship. It focused on sharing together in teaching, eating, praising God, praying, and responding to each other's needs. This fellowship was so attractive to other people that their numbers grew quite rapidly.

v. 42　These four components of the church's life may represent what occurred at their gatherings. **apostles' teaching**... The word "apostle" literally means "one sent out," and refers to those sent out to minister in Jesus name. Generally the word is also limited to those who saw Jesus face to face. Paul claimed the position of an apostle by virtue of having seen the risen Christ in a vision on the road to Damascus. The other apostles were the ones, who traveled with Jesus during his earthly ministry. Since they had this direct experience with him, their teaching was considered the most orthodox and valid. **fellowship**... Lit. "sharing." While this may include the aspect of sharing to meet material needs (v. 45), it most likely means their common participation in the Spirit as they worshiped together (1 Cor. 12). **the breaking of bread**... The Lord's Supper, in which they remembered his death (Lk. 22:19) and recognized his presence among them (Lk. 24:30–31). **to prayer**... Lit. "the prayers." This may refer to specific times and forms of prayer (as was the practice of the Jews).

vv. 43–47　The picture of the church is one of continual growth (vv. 43, 47), marked by generous sharing (vv. 44–45) and joyful worship and fellowship (vv. 46–47). Worship at the Temple continued as before since the line dividing Christianity from Judaism had not yet been drawn.

v. 43　**miraculous signs**... For examples of these, see Acts 3:1–10; 5:12–16; and 12:1–19.

v. 45　**as he had need**... Their giving was need-centered, and many in the early church needed the basics of food and shelter. This was because the church grew very rapidly among the poor, not the rich.

v. 46　**temple courts**... Christians went to the Temple because they still considered themselves to be good Jews. It wasn't until later that Christianity began to be seen as a separate religion. Nevertheless, the heart of their fellowship was not what happened in the Temple, but what happened in their homes. It was there that they had small group experiences (like eating, praying, and sharing together) that built their strong fellowship.

SESSION 2

My Story

PURPOSE: To learn the importance of my story, and the value of the single life.

AGENDA: Gathering ⬡ Bible Study ♡ Caring Time

GATHERING / 10 Minutes / All Together

Leader: Read the instructions for Step One and set the pace by going first. Then read Step Two and move on to the Bible study.

OPEN

Step One: SNAPSHOTS IN MY LIFE. We are going to share a few snapshots from our lives with other group members. Share your response to two or three of the following snapshots of your life. Be brief so everyone has a turn.

- ❏ my favorite television program as a kid
- ❏ my best subject in school
- ❏ my first pet
- ❏ my least favorite chore
- ❏ my first big trip/vacation
- ❏ my favorite room in the house
- ❏ the time I played hooky from school
- ❏ my hero at age 12
- ❏ my favorite dessert as a kid
- ❏ what I wanted to be when I grew up

INTRODUCTION

Step Two: MY STORY. We all have a story to tell. Not just a funny story from our childhood or a dramatic story from our adulthood, but a life story. All of our experiences, feelings, dreams, hopes, desires, fears, and secrets make up our life story. Although the details are different, the themes are similar.

As we open ourselves up and share our story with others, a few things will happen: 1) We will see that we really aren't as different from everyone else as we had first thought. 2) As we share our stories, we encourage others to share their stories. 3) We can all learn from each other and be encouraged by each other's stories. 4) We are drawn closer to each other as we share and listen.

11

The more comfortable we are with ourselves, the more we are able to open up to others. Self-awareness always precedes self-disclosure.

LEADER: Choose the Track One Bible study (below) or the Track Two study (page 15).

In this session, you will have a chance to share your own story. The Track One study from Luke's Gospel (which focuses on the story of the Prodigal Son) is for beginner groups. The Track Two study from Paul's second letter to the Corinthians (in which we examine some strengths and struggles in Paul's story) is for more advanced groups. Both tracks use a questionnaire approach to sharing that permits you to choose between multiple-choice options—with no right or wrong answers.

BIBLE STUDY / 30 Minutes / Groups of 4

Leader: Help the group make a decision for Track One or Track Two. If there are 7 or more in your group, quickly subdivide into 4's, and rearrange your chairs so that everyone can participate in the Bible study and discussion. Ask one person in each foursome to be the Convener, and complete the Bible study in the time allowed. Then regather for the Caring Time, allowing 20 minutes.

Leaving Home
Luke 15:11–32

STUDY

Read Luke 15:11–32 and discuss your responses to the following questions with your group. This story, popularly known as the story of the Prodigal Son, is the classic story of God's willingness to forgive us when we have chosen a barren, self-centered path. See the Reference Notes on pages 17–18 for help with a difficult phrase or word.

[11] *Jesus continued: "There was a man who had two sons.* [12] *The younger one said to his father, 'Father, give me my share of the estate.' So he divided his property between them.*

[13] *"Not long after that, the younger son got together all he had, set off for a distant country and there squandered his wealth in wild living.* [14] *After he had spent everything, there was a severe famine in that whole country, and he began to be in need.* [15] *So he went and hired himself out to a citizen of that country, who sent him to his fields to feed pigs.* [16] *He longed to fill his stomach with the pods that the pigs were eating, but no one gave him anything.*

[17] *"When he came to his senses, he said, 'How many of my father's hired men have food to spare, and here I am starving to death!* [18] *I will set out and go back to my father and say to him: Father, I have sinned against heaven and against you.* [19] *I am no longer worthy to be called your son; make me like one of your hired men.'* [20] *So he got up and went to his father.*

"But while he was still a long way off, his father saw him and was filled with compassion for him; he ran to his son, threw his arms around him and kissed him.

[21] *"The son said to him, 'Father, I have sinned against heaven and against you. I am no longer worthy to be called your son.'*

²² "But the father said to his servants, 'Quick! Bring the best robe and put it on him. Put a ring on his finger and sandals on his feet. ²³ Bring the fattened calf and kill it. Let's have a feast and celebrate. ²⁴ For this son of mine was dead and is alive again; he was lost and is found.' So they began to celebrate.

²⁵ "Meanwhile, the older son was in the field. When he came near the house, he heard music and dancing. ²⁶ So he called one of the servants and asked him what was going on. ²⁷ 'Your brother has come,' he replied, 'and your father has killed the fattened calf because he has him back safe and sound.'

²⁸ "The older brother became angry and refused to go in. So his father went out and pleaded with him. ²⁹ But he answered his father, 'Look! All these years I've been slaving for you and never disobeyed your orders. Yet you never gave me even a young goat so I could celebrate with my friends. ³⁰ But when this son of yours who has squandered your property with prostitutes comes home, you kill the fattened calf for him!'

³¹ " 'My son,' the father said, 'you are always with me, and everything I have is yours. ³² But we had to celebrate and be glad, because this brother of yours was dead and is alive again; he was lost and is found.' "

Luke 15:11–32, NIV

1. If you were to project yourself into this story, which character would you identify with most?
   - ❏ the younger son—I've squandered my allowance (and sown a few wild oats!)
   - ❏ the older son—I've been the "good kid" who did what I was told
   - ❏ the waiting father—I've had to be patient with a few prodigals in my life
   - ❏ the pigs—I've been with a few prodigals who hit bottom
   - ❏ the servant—I've been the liaison between people in conflict

2. Why did the younger son leave home in the first place?
   - ❏ he wanted to party
   - ❏ he was tired of being told what to do
   - ❏ he thought he was more mature than he was
   - ❏ he wasn't considerate of the needs of the family
   - ❏ he had to try his own wings and make his own mistakes
   - ❏ he wasn't into delayed gratification

3. Why did the older brother stay home?
   - ❏ he was too chicken to do anything else
   - ❏ he loved his father
   - ❏ he was smarter financially—he wanted to build the business
   - ❏ he believed that obedience would be rewarded
   - ❏ he was a workaholic

4. How do you react to the father's welcoming of the younger son?
   - ❏ he was foolish—the son will just be irresponsible again
   - ❏ he was unfair—the older son was right
   - ❏ he was the kind of father I wish I had
   - ❏ he was the kind of father I had

"A vital fringe benefit of being a Christian is the tremendous sense of identity that grows out of knowing Jesus Christ."
—James Dobson

13

5. If you were the older son, what would you do next?
   - ❑ go off on my own partying binge
   - ❑ go in and join my father's party
   - ❑ stay outside and sulk for the rest of my life
   - ❑ go in and ruin the party for everyone else
   - ❑ go back to work and try not to think about it
   - ❑ other: _____

6. How does the prodigal's leaving home compare to your own experience of leaving home?
   - ❑ what leaving home experience?—I'm still there!
   - ❑ I left home under conflict and tension, as did he
   - ❑ I left home for fun and freedom, as did he
   - ❑ I left home because I was forced to
   - ❑ I left home with good feelings and the support of family
   - ❑ other: _____

7. Who has played "the older brother" in your life—the one who was always jealous whenever anything good happened to you?
   - ❑ an older brother or sister
   - ❑ a younger brother or sister
   - ❑ a parent
   - ❑ my ex-spouse
   - ❑ a co-worker
   - ❑ a "friend"
   - ❑ no one
   - ❑ other: _____

8. Who has played the role of the "waiting father"—the one who has always forgiven and been patient of you?
   - ❑ my father
   - ❑ my mother
   - ❑ a grandparent
   - ❑ my brother
   - ❑ my sister
   - ❑ a friend
   - ❑ God alone
   - ❑ no one

9. If you were to have a party to celebrate the most positive relationship you have had so far, what relationship would that be?

10. If you could talk to your father or mother right now, what would you want to say to them about the time when you left home?
    - ❑ I wouldn't talk with them
    - ❑ I'm sorry!
    - ❑ I'm no longer worthy to be called your son/daughter
    - ❑ thanks!
    - ❑ can't we just party together and forget the past?
    - ❑ I still need you!
    - ❑ other: _____

LEADER: When you have completed the Bible study, move on to the Caring Time (page 16).

14

Track 2

My Strengths and Stresses
2 Corinthians 11:21–31

STUDY

Read 2 Corinthians 11:21–31 and share your responses to the following questions with your group. Paul wrote this in response to finding that some people had come to Corinth bragging about themselves and putting down Paul and his authority. If you do not understand a word or phrase, check the Reference Notes on page 18.

What anyone else dares to boast about—I am speaking as a fool—I also dare to boast about. ²² Are they Hebrews? So am I. Are they Israelites? So am I. Are they Abraham's descendants? So am I. ²³ Are they servants of Christ? (I am out of my mind to talk like this.) I am more. I have worked much harder, been in prison more frequently, been flogged more severely, and been exposed to death again and again. ²⁴ Five times I received from the Jews the forty lashes minus one.

²⁵ Three times I was beaten with rods, once I was stoned, three times I was shipwrecked, I spent a night and a day in the open sea, ²⁶ I have been constantly on the move. I have been in danger from rivers, in danger from bandits, in danger from my own countrymen, in danger from Gentiles; in danger in the city, in danger in the country, in danger at sea; and in danger from false brothers. ²⁷ I have labored and toiled and have often gone without sleep; I have known hunger and thirst and have often gone without food; I have been cold and naked. ²⁸ Besides everything else, I face daily the pressure of my concern for all the churches. ²⁹ Who is weak, and I do not feel weak? Who is led into sin, and I do not inwardly burn?

³⁰ If I must boast, I will boast of the things that show my weakness. ³¹ The God and Father of the Lord Jesus, who is to be praised forever, knows that I am not lying.

2 Corinthians 11:21–31, NIV

> "It is not the outward storms and stresses of life that defeat and disrupt personality, but its inner conflicts and miseries. If a [person] is happy and stable at heart, he can normally cope, even with zest, with difficulties that lie outside his personality."
> —J.B. Phillips

1. If you hadn't heard of Paul the Apostle before, what would be your initial impression of him from this passage?
   ☐ he's boastful
   ☐ he has deep convictions
   ☐ he is temperamental
   ☐ he is overly worried about being considered boastful
   ☐ he is fearless
   ☐ he is defensive
   ☐ he cares about people
   ☐ he's got a martyr complex
   ☐ other: _____

2. If you had been in Corinth, which of the "credentials" that Paul used to defend himself would you have been the most impressed with?
   ☐ his "roots," his ancestry (v. 22)
   ☐ his dedication to Christ (v. 23)
   ☐ his willingness to risk and sacrifice (vv. 23–27)
   ☐ his empathy for those in his churches (vv. 28–29)

3. What do you know of your "roots"? From which countries and cultures did your ancestors come? Do you know of any famous or particularly interesting ancestors?

4. What quality do you think you received from a parent or grandparent that would be considered a strength?

5. How comfortable are you when talking about your strengths and talents?
   - ❏ like Paul—all of that is boasting
   - ❏ ambivalent—I can do it, but sometimes I feel uncomfortable
   - ❏ comfortable—it's part of sharing who I am
   - ❏ great—it gives me a good feeling
   - ❏ what strengths and talents?

6. Find and share two of the following stresses that, like Paul's struggles, helped to form who you are:
   - ❏ the death of a parent or loved one as a child
   - ❏ coming from a dysfunctional family
   - ❏ a learning disability
   - ❏ a financial loss
   - ❏ being an "army brat"
   - ❏ extreme shyness
   - ❏ other: _____
   - ❏ the divorce of my parents
   - ❏ health problems
   - ❏ a physical disability
   - ❏ being the victim of a crime
   - ❏ being a "PK" (preacher's kid)
   - ❏ my own divorce
   - ❏ a professional failure
   - ❏ death of a loved one as an adult

7. Which of your strengths helped pull you through that time?

8. What dangers are you most concerned about right now?
   - ❏ crime, violence, and the dangers in our society
   - ❏ cancer, AIDS, and other health dangers
   - ❏ recession, fluctuating stock market and other economic dangers
   - ❏ pornography, commercialism, and other moral dangers

LEADER: When you have completed the Bible study, move on to the Caring Time (below).

9. What strength do you have to withstand those dangers?

CARING TIME / 20 Minutes / All Together

Leader: The purpose of the Caring Time in this session is to spend time in caring support for each other through Sharing, Prayer, and Action.

SHARING

Have each person in the group finish this sentence:

> *"If I could use a little extra strength for something right now, it would be for...."*

PRAYER

Close with a short time of prayer, focusing on what people shared above. Go around in a circle and give everyone an opportunity to pray. If you want to pray in silence when it is your turn, say the word "Amen" when you have finished your prayer, so that the next person will know when to start.

ACTION

On an index card, write your first name and one prayer request you have about being single. Randomly distribute the cards, and ask everyone to pray for the person on their card throughout the coming week.

v. 12 give me my share… Under Jewish law, the younger of two sons would receive one-third of the estate upon his father's death (Dt. 21:17). Even though a father could divide up his property before he died, this son's request would be considered unbelievably callous. It implies that the fact his father is alive interferes with his plans. The father willingly divides the property between his sons. The expectation is that while the land legally belongs to the sons, they are morally obliged to provide for their father while he is alive.

v. 13 got together all he had… The younger son sold off his share of the estate, so that he could have cash to do what he wanted! This act was scandalous, since a person's identity and future was tied to his family's land. By selling it off, he separated himself from his family, lost his means of income, and robbed future children of the security of having land.

vv. 15–16 pigs… To Jews, pigs were ceremonially unclean animals (Lev. 11:7) and they would not eat, raise, or touch them. So he was working for a Gentile. **the pods**… While eating the food of pigs sounds terrible even to modern readers, it would have been utterly horrifying to the Pharisees. Jesus has painted a picture of an unbelievably arrogant, unpleasant, dislikable, immoral, foolish, and irreligious young man.

v. 17 he came to his senses… He changed his mind (see also Lk. 18:4). The phrase does not indicate repentance as we would understand it, but simply a recognition that the way he chose is not working.

v. 19 no longer worthy… The son realized that his careless attitude toward his father meant he had no legal, moral, or relational claim on his father's goodwill. **hired men**… He simply hopes to be treated as well as the lowliest day-to-day worker on his father's farm.

v. 20 filled with compassion… There is no haughtiness of wounded pride, but only the welling up of pity, love, and joy. **ran to his son**… Social customs dictated that it was degrading for an elderly man to run to anyone, especially to someone who had disgraced him. The father should have turned his back on this son. This picture presents an absolutely unique and staggering insight into God's response to a repentant sinner. **kissed him**… Although this is a typical greeting for men, it would have been inappropriate (given the son's grave offense against his father).

v. 21 I am no longer worthy to be called your son… Most commentators suggest that the father interrupts his son's memorized speech, but Bailey notes that the father's action may have so moved the son that he realized the enormity of his actions. Now he reflects a true sense of repentance—offering nothing except a contrite spirit.

v. 22 the best robe… This was a sign that people should honor the son as they honor the father. **a ring**… A signet ring used to seal official documents, giving the son the authority to represent the father. **sandals**… Being shoeless was a sign of a slave. Thus the son is *immediately* and *unconditionally* elevated to a position of honor and respect in the home.

v. 23 fattened calf… When an animal was slaughtered for a special guest, its blood was sprinkled on the threshold of the home. Stepping over the blood into the home was a sign of a covenant between guest and host (Bailey). Here it indicates a new covenant of love between the father and his son.

v. 28–30 This son's refusal to enter the house was a sign of grave disrespect for his father, since he was expected to be a gracious host. As with the younger son, the father "went out" to meet his son and "plead with him." While the father's love wrought humility in the younger son, the older son responds with even more insulting behavior. **I've been slaving for you**... He apparently viewed things in terms of a master/slave relationship and never enjoyed the relationship with his father that was available to him. **you never gave me**... He ignores that he has always been in the position to enjoy the love of his father, whereas the younger son has not. **this son of yours**... A derisive way of avoiding his relationship with his younger brother.

vv. 31–32 The father pleads with him to see things differently. **everything I have is yours**... This assures the older son that his inheritance is secure despite the presence of his younger brother. The father does not see his older son as a servant, but as an heir. Jesus purposely left the story open-ended to force the Pharisees to fill in the ending by their behavior. If they continue to reject those whom God receives, then they show that they never knew the Father's heart at all.

Summary... In 11:1–15, Paul pinpointed the danger that the false apostles pose to the Christian church. They are, in fact, preaching a different Jesus, a different spirit, and a different gospel. They are succeeding with this because of their supposed qualifications "which... consisted of commendation from high authority, impressive speech and behavior, and manifestations of the Spirit..." (Barrett). Thus it is here that Paul (against his will) boasts of his own credentials!

v. 22 Paul begins his boasting by pointing out that no matter what standard is used, he is as Jewish as it is possible to be: i.e., the false apostles from Jerusalem cannot claim to be better Jews than he—which would undercut their claim to be preaching a "purer" gospel. **Hebrews**... Paul is a pure-blooded Jew. He is not a convert or a half-Jew (with only one Jewish parent). **Israelites**... He was brought up in the Jewish religion and culture. **Abraham's descendants**... Such folk are part of God's chosen people.

vv. 23–28 Having listed his Jewish credentials, Paul turns next to his qualifications as a Christian: he has suffered greatly as a servant of Christ. As a pioneer missionary, his life has been filled with danger and hard work.

v. 25 **beaten with rods**... This is how the Romans administered punishment **stoned**... See Acts 14:19. **shipwrecked**... See Acts 27:14–44 (though this incident had not yet occurred when Paul wrote 2 Corinthians. Since Paul traveled frequently by ship (and since shipwrecks were common in those days), it seems that Paul endured at least two shipwrecks.

v. 26 Having recalled the shipwreck, Paul now describes other dangers that travelers faced. **rivers**... Not all rivers had bridges or safe ferries. **bandits**... This would have been a special problem when Paul transported collections (which were given to help poorer churches). **in danger from my own countrymen**... Such danger came from mobs, from the courts, and from personal attacks.

v. 29 **weak**... Paul's emphasis throughout this section has been on his weakness—his unimpressive speech, his poor appearance, his poverty—in which he glories. It is through these things that Christ's power is revealed. In his "boasting," he now boasts of being weakest of all! **inwardly burn**... In his concern for the churches, a constant source of anguish is over those who have been led astray from the faith.

**REFERENCE NOTES:
2 CORINTHIANS
11:21–31**

SESSION 3

Choices

PURPOSE: To understand the value of friendships and to start building a relationship with others in your group.

AGENDA: ♡ Gathering 📖 Bible Study ♡ Caring Time

OPEN

GATHERING / 10 Minutes / All Together

Leader: The purpose of the Gathering time is to break the ice. Read the instructions for Step One and go first. Then read the Introduction (Step Two) and the instructions for the Bible study.

Step One: QUIZ SHOW. You have all been chosen to participate on the latest TV quiz show. This is your chance to reveal some of your most interesting characteristics and to win some big bucks (funny money) by predicting what your friends are likely to do and choose. Like a TV quiz show, someone from the group picks a category from the six choices available and reads the $1 question. The others in the group guess out loud what the answer will be. Then the person explains his/her answer and those that guessed right put $1 in the margin for their score. Then the person reads the $2 question, and the others guess, etc., until the person has read all the questions in that category. Another person chooses a different category, and the process is repeated until everyone has read a category. The person with the most money at the end wins. To get started, have the host or hostess who's invited you to their house go first by reading the ENTERTAINMENT category. There are more categories on the next page.

ENTERTAINMENT

For $1: I would likely:
- ☐ go out for a first-run movie
- ☐ stay home and rent a video

For $3: Concerning movies, I prefer:
- ☐ comedy
- ☐ shoot-'em-up action
- ☐ horror film
- ☐ serious drama
- ☐ love story
- ☐ science fiction

For $2: On TV, I would choose:
- ☐ a police drama
- ☐ the Evening News
- ☐ a talk show
- ☐ a soap opera
- ☐ a sitcom

For $4: If the movie gets scary, I will probably:
- ☐ go to the bathroom
- ☐ close my eyes and peek
- ☐ slink into my chair
- ☐ clutch my friend
- ☐ soak it in from the edge of my seat

TASTES

For $1: In music, I am closer to:
- [ ] Mozart
- [ ] 10,000 Maniacs

For $2: In furniture, I prefer:
- [ ] early American
- [ ] French provincial
- [ ] Scandinavian
- [ ] hodgepodge—little of everything

For $3: My choice for reading material is:
- [ ] science fiction
- [ ] romance
- [ ] biography
- [ ] mystery
- [ ] novel

For $4: If I had $1,000 to splurge, I would buy:
- [ ] artwork
- [ ] mutual fund investment
- [ ] update my wardrobe
- [ ] CD's and movies
- [ ] new stereo equipment

HABITS

For $1: I am more likely to take:
- [ ] a shower
- [ ] a bath

For $2: I am more likely to squeeze the toothpaste:
- [ ] in the middle
- [ ] from the end
- [ ] roll it up from the end

For $3: I'm likely to read the Sunday paper starting with (pick two):
- [ ] the funnies
- [ ] sports
- [ ] world news
- [ ] local news
- [ ] the society page
- [ ] business

For $4: When I undress at night, I put my clothes:
- [ ] on a hanger in the closet
- [ ] folded neatly over a chair
- [ ] stuffed into the hamper
- [ ] tossed in a corner
- [ ] on the floor where I stepped out of them

FOOD

For $1: I am more likely to pick:
- [ ] a gourmet meal
- [ ] meat and potatoes

For $2: When eating chicken, I pick first:
- [ ] a drumstick
- [ ] a breast
- [ ] a thigh

For $3: When dining out, I would go to:
- [ ] a small, intimate inn
- [ ] a crowded club
- [ ] a sidewalk café
- [ ] an expensive restaurant
- [ ] a drive-thru fast-food place

For $4: I draw the line when it comes to eating:
- [ ] frogs legs
- [ ] raw oysters
- [ ] sweetbread
- [ ] snails
- [ ] pickled pigs feet
- [ ] Rocky Mountain oysters

CLOTHES

For $1: For clothes, I would go to:
- [ ] Sears
- [ ] Saks Fifth Avenue

For $2: I feel more comfortable wearing:
- [ ] formal clothes
- [ ] casual clothes
- [ ] jeans
- [ ] grubbies

For $3: In buying clothes, I look first for:
- [ ] fashion/style
- [ ] price
- [ ] brand name
- [ ] quality

For $4: In buying clothes, I usually:
- [ ] shop all day for a bargain
- [ ] go to one store, but try on everything
- [ ] buy the first thing I try on
- [ ] buy without trying it on
- [ ] wait for a sale

Step Two: CHOICES. The freedom to choose is one of our most precious freedoms. Isn't that what we say America is all about? Isn't that what many have fought and died for? But freedom to choose also has its down side—namely, that when we are free to choose for ourselves, we must also take the responsibility for our choices. Sometimes that is difficult to do. Being responsible for our choices means having to deal with guilt when we make wrong moral choices. It means having to deal with frustration and anger at ourselves when our choices lead us down fruitless paths. It means having to deal with our own uncertainties and insecurities when we are trying to make decisions. What if I marry and he/she is the wrong person? What if I buy this house and find it was a bad investment? What if I choose a profession, invest in an education, and then it turns out all wrong for me?

The responsibility that goes with decision-making is why many people really don't want to make their own choices. Psychiatrist Erich Fromm wrote a classic book called *Escape from Freedom,* in which he said that people choose individuals like Adolph Hitler to lead them because these leaders will make decisions for them (people do this and therefore they won't have to take responsibility for themselves).

It's not necessary for us to "escape from freedom" if we can learn to use our freedom wisely in the choices we make. That is what this session is about. In Track One (from Mark's Gospel), we will consider what it says about the choices Jesus made about (1) who he would serve, (2) where he would live, (3) what he would do, and (4) who his friends would be. Since these are some of the same choices we have, this track will help us to think through these choices as well. In Track Two (from Paul's first letter to the Corinthians), we will look more specifically at the choice of being single, and Paul's discussion of that choice.

LEADER: Choose the Track One Bible study (below) or the Track Two study (page 24).

BIBLE STUDY / 30 Minutes / Groups of 4

Leader: Help the group decide to choose Track One or Track Two for their Bible study. If there are 7 or more in the group, encourage them to move into groups of four. Ask one person in each group to be the Convener. The Convener guides the sharing and makes sure that each group member has an opportunity to answer each question.

A World of Choices
Mark 1:9–20

STUDY

Read Mark 1:9–20 and share your answers to the following questions with your group. This passage is about the beginning of Jesus' ministry, when he was about thirty years old. Check the Reference Notes on pages 27–28 if you have questions about a word or phrase.

⁹ At that time Jesus came from Nazareth in Galilee and was baptized by John in tl Jordan. ¹⁰ As Jesus was coming up out of the water, he saw heaven being torn open a the Spirit descending on him like a dove. ¹¹ And a voice came from heaven: "You are m Son, whom I love; with you I am well pleased."

¹² At once the Spirit sent him out into the desert, ¹³ and he was in the desert forty day being tempted by Satan. He was with the wild animals, and angels attended him.

¹⁴ After John was put in prison, Jesus went into Galilee, proclaiming the good news God. ¹⁵ "The time has come," he said. "The kingdom of God is near. Repent and belie the good news!"

¹⁶ As Jesus walked beside the Sea of Galilee, he saw Simon and his brother Andre casting a net into the lake, for they were fishermen. ¹⁷ "Come, follow me," Jesus sai "and I will make you fishers of men." ¹⁸ At once they left their nets and followed hin

¹⁹ When he had gone a little farther, he saw James son of Zebedee and his brother Joh in a boat, preparing their nets. ²⁰ Without delay he called them, and they left their fathe Zebedee in the boat with the hired men and followed him.

Mark 1:9–20, NI

1. From the picture of Jesus in this passage, choose three of the following words which you believe best describe him:

   ❐ visionary ❐ obedient
   ❐ fearless ❐ uninhibited
   ❐ audacious ❐ interfering
   ❐ commanding ❐ charismatic
   ❐ confident ❐ focused
   ❐ spiritual ❐ reclusive
   ❐ domineering ❐ positive

2. Why did the voice of God say, "You are my Son, whom I love; with you I am well pleased"?

   ❐ Jesus didn't know he was God's Son until then
   ❐ God wanted to affirm the choice Jesus had made
   ❐ God wanted the people around to know this was his Son
   ❐ to serve as an example so we will affirm others

3. As a child, when did a parent tell you how "well-pleased" they were with something you had done, or a decision you had made?

   ❐ they never affirmed me
   ❐ when I came home with good grades
   ❐ when I did well in sports or a school activity
   ❐ when I was baptized or confirmed
   ❐ all the time
   ❐ other: _____

4. What is the significance of the fact that Jesus was in the desert forty days being tempted by Satan?

   ❐ he had to be put to the test before entering his time of ministry
   ❐ he had to see what other choices were available before telling others to choose God
   ❐ it was symbolic of the temptation he experienced all of his life
   ❐ he had to know what it was like for us to be tempted

5. In the desert Jesus was "with the wild animals." What "wild animals" have harassed you the most in your life?
   - ❏ two-legged ones who lurk in singles' bars
   - ❏ the "sharks" in the world of my chosen profession
   - ❏ the beasts who live in the shadows of my childhood memories
   - ❏ some "rats" I have chosen as friends
   - ❏ the monster I sometimes am

6. Who were the "angels" who attended you (v. 13) during your crisis times in life? What were their names? What did they do that was particularly supportive and helpful?

7. Which of the following describes the method you think Jesus used in choosing his disciples?
   - ❏ he chose them at random
   - ❏ he looked for hard-working people
   - ❏ he probably knew them well before calling them in these verses
   - ❏ he felt a kind of "chemistry" with them
   - ❏ he used supernatural insight

*"The deepest need
of man
is the need
to overcome
his separateness,
to leave the prison
of his aloneness."
—Erich Fromm*

8. What criteria do you use in choosing your friends?
   - ❏ I take anyone who will have me
   - ❏ I look for a "chemistry" between us
   - ❏ I look for someone who is easy to talk to
   - ❏ I look for someone who has similar interests to mine
   - ❏ I look for someone who can help my career
   - ❏ I look for someone who I can trust
   - ❏ I look for someone who has a good sense of humor
   - ❏ other: _____

9. Of the following decisions Jesus made in this passage, which do you have the hardest time making?
   - ❏ who I serve (vv. 9–11)
   - ❏ where to live and work (v. 14)
   - ❏ what my mission or role is in life (v. 15)
   - ❏ who to choose as my friends (vv. 16–20)

10. On the scale below, indicate the amount of help you think you need to make the big decisions in life:

**LEADER: When you
have completed the
Bible study, move on
to the Caring Time
(page 27).**

1	2	3	4	5	6	7	8	9	10
NONE—I'm doing fine on my own!				**I'll get by with a little help from my friends!**				**Someone PLEASE tell me what to do!**	

23

Jesus' life was filled with choices. His choices reflected God's will in his life. During his time in the desert, Jesus was tempted with the choices of having his immediate needs met or power. Christ will help us to make the right choice whenever we face temptation.

Following his time in the desert, Jesus chose his disciples. The people he chose were not the most likely candidates. Jesus did not choose powerful or popular people. Nor did he choose men who were wealthy or well-connected. Instead he chose men with simple means and with simple faith—men chosen not because of their credentials, but because of their potential. Jesus saw the rough edges, but he also saw their hearts. Seeing past someone's credentials to their potential is an excellent guideline for us to use in choosing our friends as well.

The Single Advantage
1 Corinthians 7:8–9, 25–35

STUDY

Read 1 Corinthians 7:8–9, 25–35 and discuss the questions which follow with your group. This passage is part of the instructions the Apostle Paul wrote to the church in Corinth in regard to marriage. If you have difficulty with a word or phrase, consult the Reference Notes on pages 28–29.

⁸ Now to the unmarried and the widows I say: It is good for them to stay unmarried, as I am. ⁹ But if they cannot control themselves, they should marry, for it is better to marry than to burn with passion.

²⁵ Now about virgins: I have no command from the Lord, but I give a judgment as one who by the Lord's mercy is trustworthy. ²⁶ Because of the present crisis, I think that it is good for you to remain as you are. ²⁷ Are you married? Do not seek a divorce. Are you unmarried? Do not look for a wife. ²⁸ But if you do marry, you have not sinned; and if a virgin marries, she has not sinned. But those who marry will face many troubles in this life, and I want to spare you this.

²⁹ What I mean, brothers, is that the time is short. From now on those who have wives should live as if they had none; ³⁰ those who mourn, as if they did not; those who are happy, as if they were not; those who buy something, as if it were not theirs to keep; ³¹ those who use the things of the world, as if not engrossed in them. For this world in its present form is passing away.

³² I would like you to be free from concern. An unmarried man is concerned about the Lord's affairs—how he can please the Lord. ³³ But a married man is concerned about the affairs of this world—how he can please his wife— ³⁴ and his interests are divided. An unmarried woman or virgin is concerned about the Lord's affairs: Her aim is to be devoted to the Lord in both body and spirit. But a married woman is concerned about the affairs of this world—how she can please her husband. ³⁵ I am saying this for your own good, not to restrict you, but that you may live in a right way in undivided devotion to the Lord.

1 Corinthians 7:8–9, 25–35, NIV

1. If Paul had his own "advice column" today and he wrote this advice to someone, what headline do you think it should be given?
   - ☐ "Being Single Isn't for Wimps," advises Paul
   - ☐ "Stay Focused—Stay Single," Paul declares
   - ☐ "Marital Status not the Main Issue," states Paul
   - ☐ "Paul Steers Singles Away from Worry—and Marriage!"

2. Which of these phrases best summarizes Paul's attitude toward marriage in this passage?
   - ☐ it's more trouble than it's worth
   - ☐ it takes too much time and energy for a Christian
   - ☐ it's basically for those who can't control their sexual desire
   - ☐ it dilutes a person's devotion to God

3. Paul seems to think that married people have more worries and concerns than singles. In today's world, how would you compare the worries and concerns of these two lifestyles?
   - ☐ married people have far more things to worry about
   - ☐ married people have a few more things to worry about
   - ☐ married people and singles have about the same number of worries—they are simply different
   - ☐ single people have a few more things to worry about
   - ☐ single people have far more worries and concerns than do married people

4. What is your biggest worry about being single?
   - ☐ that I will never get married
   - ☐ working full time and caring for children by myself
   - ☐ finances!
   - ☐ that people will think something is wrong with me because I'm not married
   - ☐ loneliness
   - ☐ resolving sexual tensions in a Christian way
   - ☐ other: _____

5. What do you think is the greatest advantage to being single?
   - ☐ more freedom
   - ☐ fewer arguments
   - ☐ not having to share my space
   - ☐ nobody I have to answer to at home
   - ☐ more time for God
   - ☐ financial independence
   - ☐ more time for friendship development
   - ☐ other: _____

"No one can develop freely in this world or find a full life without feeling understood by at least one person."
—Paul Tournier

6. How convinced are you by Paul's argument that single people are more focused on serving God?
   - ☐ totally—that's why Catholic priests don't marry!
   - ☐ mostly convinced—singles have much more volunteer time
   - ☐ only partially—it depends on the individual
   - ☐ not at all—singles focus on friends and dating
   - ☐ not at all—singles focus on their problems

7. As a single, how could you use your time and freedom to serve God and others?
   - ☐ spend more time in prayer
   - ☐ volunteer more at church
   - ☐ get involved in a project to help those in need
   - ☐ do more visiting of shut-ins and new people in town
   - ☐ other: _____

LEADER: When you have completed the Bible study, move on to the Caring Time (page 27).

8. What obstacle might prevent you from using your time and freedom in the way you mentioned in question 7?

COMMENT

Our world today is quite different than Paul's. But the two main reasons Paul gives to the Corinthians for staying single are valid in today's world as well.

Paul makes it very clear that he believes the single state is to be preferred over marriage. Undoubtedly, many in our society would find that hard to accept today. Paul's first reason is that the world as we know it is passing away. Since Paul believed that Christ's return was near, everything needed to be put aside (including marriage) in order to work for God's kingdom. This ties in with his second reason for preferring singleness. Singleness is better because it allows a person to devote more time and energy to serving Christ.

We all have our reasons for being single. And although our reasons may not be the same as Paul's, he gives us some food for thought.

CARING TIME / 20 Minutes / All Together

Leader: Bring all the foursomes back together for a time of caring. Follow the three steps below.

SHARING

Share with the group a choice that you will be making in the next few weeks in one or two of the following areas:

- ❏ at your job
- ❏ financially
- ❏ in your lifestyle
- ❏ in a relationship with a family member
- ❏ in a romantic relationship
- ❏ in relation to a spiritual matter

PRAYER

Close with a short time of prayer, remembering the choices group members will be making. If you would like to pray in silence, say the word "Amen" when you have finished your prayer, so that the next person will know when to start.

ACTION

One day this week, take a little notebook with you and write down every enjoyable thing you experience. Put a little exclamation mark by any of these which you might not have been able to experience if you were not single. At the end of the day, thank God for all of these experiences and for the opportunities available to you as a single person.

REFERENCE NOTES:
MARK 1:9–20

v. 9 In the midst of this supercharged atmosphere Jesus starts his ministry. The subsequent drama of his baptism and temptation (vv. 9–13) bring into this already impressive scene a supernatural host—God the Father, God the Holy Spirit, and God the Son (v. 11), as well as angels and Satan himself (v. 13). **baptized**... By allowing himself to be baptized, Jesus identified with the people of Israel and with their sin. Although he himself was without sin (1 Pet. 2:22), he foreshadowed his eventual death for sin.

v. 11 **a voice**... These words from God combine phrases from Psalm 2:7 (which speaks of Israel's King as God's royal Son) and Isaiah 42:1 (which speaks of the suffering servant of God). In the Gospel, Jesus is pictured as the Son of God who came to serve his people. These words are God's unqualified affirmation of Jesus as he begins his ministry.

v. 12 **the Spirit sent him**... The same Spirit who had come to Jesus in such affirming power now sends him forth to this time of testing.

v. 13 **forty days. . . tempted**... After Israel was delivered from Egypt, the people spent forty days in the wilderness. During this time they rebelled against God and failed to trust in his promises (Num. 14:26–35). In alluding to this Mark indicates that Jesus was also tested for forty days, but came through without rebelling. Thus he was uniquely prepared to obey God's will in a way Israel as a nation never did. **wild animals**... This may have been written to reassure Christians (who were actually facing wild beasts in the Roman Coliseum) that Jesus identified with their trials and sufferings.

v. 14 **After John was put in prison**... There is a gap of perhaps a year between the incidents recorded in vv. 9–13 and those recorded here. **Galilee**... This was the northern province of Palestine, about twenty-five by thirty-five miles in size. Galilee had a population of approximately three hundred and fifty thousand, one hundred thousand of whom were Jews.

The Jewish population was considered ignorant and lax when it came to religious matters by those who lived in Jerusalem.

v. 15 **The time has come**... God's kingdom, which had been long-awaited, was now declared to be at hand. **kingdom of God**... The Jews regarded themselves as God's special people. He alone was their King. But, in fact, they were under the domination of Rome with Caesar as their king. Still, they awaited the day when the Messiah (a warrior-king with invincible power) would arise to lead Israel to military victory and establish Jerusalem as the capitol of the world. It would take Jesus' entire ministry to show that he was not this sort of Messiah, and that his kingdom was of a very different nature.

v. 17 In asking these men to follow him, Jesus was inviting them to join his band of disciples. Simon and Andrew would have been familiar with rabbis who had small groups of followers. In telling them he would make them "fishers of men," Jesus defined their task by using a metaphor they understood: they would seek converts to his teaching.

v. 18 **At once they left**... Jesus had been preaching in Galilee and these fishermen had probably heard his message prior to their call. Still, their action took great faith and courage. Such people generally lived where they were born, stayed with their families and took up their father's occupation.

v. 20 **the hired men**... James and John perhaps came from a wealthier family than Simon and Andrew.

v. 8 **The unmarried**... This was ordinarily used for "widowers." **stay unmarried**... Paul does not object to marriage, but acknowledges the benefits of singleness (see vv. 32–34). **as I am**... It is likely that Paul was a widower (or a divorcé) himself, since Jewish men were expected to marry.

v. 9 **cannot control themselves**... Lit. "if they do not exercise self-control." Formerly-married Christians who want to be sexually active ought to feel free to remarry. There is no particular merit in trying to remain unmarried when one really desires a sexual union.

vv. 25–40 Having addressed the married and widowed, Paul now focuses primarily on those who have never married. His preference for the single state is clear. This is not because it is a spiritually purer condition as the ascetic would teach (v. 1). It is because of "the present crisis" and "the time is short"—references to his belief that Christ was returning soon.

v. 25 **virgins**... Although this word applies to men or women without sexual experience, Paul uses it to refer to women. **I give a judgment**... Paul does not have a clear word from the Lord, but he does offer his own opinion, which he feels comes from the Lord (v. 40).

v. 26 **the present crisis**... Paul, like the other apostles, believed that the return of Christ to establish God's kingdom was imminent (v. 29; 1 Th. 4:15–17; although later on, church leaders realized it may be delayed far longer than they had expected—2 Pet. 3:4–9). In light of the anticipation of such a climactic event, everything else must be put aside—including the entanglements of marriage—in order to get ready for God's new order. **it is good for you to remain as you are**... This is a specific application of his general principle (vv. 17, 20, 24) to the situation of the unmarried. Just as the married should not divorce, so the unmarried should remain single (v. 27).

v. 28   **have not sinned**... The Corinthian ascetics have probably been insisting that the unmarried remain single. While Paul sees the wisdom of this, it is not a command but simply a bit of good advice (which the Christian is free to accept or reject in light of his or her situation). **many troubles**... Given Paul's anticipation of the Lord's return, he is probably thinking of the afflictions of the last days which will be especially hard on those who have families (e.g., Mk. 13:17).

v. 31   **this world . . . is passing away**... The institutions of "this age" (such as death and commerce) and structured relationships (like marriage) are passing away, now that Christ has ushered in the "new age." When his kingdom comes in fullness, there will be no more marriage (Mk. 12:25).

v. 34   **his interests are divided**... The married man is rightly concerned about how to please the Lord, and equally right in his concern to please his wife (no less could be expected of a Christian husband). This is the problem: how to be faithful to both legitimate commitments. **a married woman**... The same is true of the married woman: her attention is divided in a way which is not true of the single woman.

v. 35   "The drift is clear: if you avoid marriage you avoid encumbrances, and you can devote yourself to the Lord's work without incurring problems, difficulties, and anxieties, which married people incur. But this is not a rule, and indeed seemliness may be transgressed by celibacy as well as by marriage (a concession the Corinthian ascetics would probably find it very difficult to allow)" (Barrett). **not to restrict you**... Literally, "not to put a halter around your neck," as one would do in order to domesticate an animal.

v. 36   **the virgin he is engaged to**... Now Paul comes to the specific problem in Corinth. As one would expect (given the maxim in verse 26), the ascetic party is urging engaged couples to forgo marriage. While Paul would agree with this advice (since he feels that the Lord may return any day), he takes great pains to show that this is not the only view, and that getting married is certainly not sinful. Paul is writing primarily to engaged couples: when he uses the word *virgin* in this passage, he is probably referring to young women engaged to be married.

v. 39   **free to marry anyone**... The Christian is not bound by the custom of levirate marriage (whereby a man marries his brother's widow in order to bear a child, who will carry the name of the deceased brother [Deut. 25:5–10]). **he must belong to the Lord**... The phrase is, literally, "only in the Lord." It is also possible to translate this phrase "remembering that she is a Christian." In any case, Christian widows (or widowers) may remarry, but must do so in the context of their commitment to Christ.

SESSION 4

Sexuality

PURPOSE: To understand the depth of human sexuality.

AGENDA: Gathering 📖 Bible Study ♡ Caring Time

GATHERING / 10 Minutes / All Together

Leader: As difficult as it is for people to share with one another, it's much more difficult for them to talk about their sexuality. Read the instructions for Step One and set the pace by going first. Then read Step Two and move on to the Bible study.

OPEN

Step One: SOME ENCHANTED EVENING. Throwing caution to the wind, what would be your idea of a perfect evening? Choose one of the following "enchanted evenings," or create your own. Share your responses with the group.

- ❏ a night on the town—complete with dinner and dancing
- ❏ a quiet evening at home in front of the fireplace, with a good book
- ❏ time with my friends
- ❏ go to the laundromat
- ❏ take in a movie or go to the theater
- ❏ rent out a nightclub for a party with 100 friends
- ❏ clean out my closets
- ❏ a romantic evening—a candlelight dinner with a special someone
- ❏ watch the game with the guys
- ❏ watch a video with my favorite pint of ice cream
- ❏ work on an unfinished project
- ❏ go to the gym and work out
- ❏ other:_____

INTRODUCTION

Step Two: SEXUALITY. In perhaps no area of life does a single person live under more pressure than in the area of sexuality. Sex is used to sell everything from automobiles to soft drinks. Most TV network prime-time shows use sex to boost their ratings, and the sexual scenes in such shows are getting bolder and bolder. Teasingly naked women are used on the cover of magazines that have not traditionally been thought of as "girlie" magazines. Women's magazines respond with pictures of "hunks" and articles on sexual technique. The end result of all of this for the single is that sex is kept forever before us, and the pressure to use others for sexual convenience is great.

In the midst of this pressure we need to be reminded of some important points. One is that God created us as sexual beings—"male and female he created them" (Gen. 1:27). That means that it is good to be sexual. But how do we express that sexuality in a responsible way? Many of us struggle with that question. When James Patterson and Peter Kim, in a study for their book *The Day America Told the Truth*, surveyed Americans on what they were most ashamed of, far and away the most frequent response had to do with sexual indiscretions. Another point to be reminded of is the need to distinguish between sexuality and sexual activity.

LEADER: Choose the Track One Bible study (below) or the Track Two study (page 34).

This session will help us to take a good look at the issue of sexuality and responsible sexual behavior. In the Track One study (from Luke's Gospel), we will consider a story about a prostitute who turned her life around for Jesus. We will also consider the role touching plays in our sexuality. In the Track Two study (from Paul's first letter to the Thessalonians), we will consider what Scripture says about responsible sexual expression.

As you share your story and struggles with sexuality, be assured that confidentiality is understood. The purpose of this Bible study is to share together and to encourage one another.

BIBLE STUDY / 30 Minutes / Groups of 4

Leader: Help the groups decide on a Track One or a Track Two Bible study. If there are more than 7 people, divide into groups of 4 and ask one person in each group to be the Convener. Finish the Bible study in 30 minutes, and gather the groups together for the Caring Time.

A Touching Act
Luke 7:36–50

STUDY

Read Luke 7:36–50 and discuss the questions which follow with your group. While Jesus is at the home of a Pharisee, a woman who is a "sinful woman" comes and wipes her tears on his feet, kisses them, and anoints them with perfume. While the Pharisees are outraged by this, Jesus accepts it as an expression of love and repentance. Use the Reference Notes on pages 36–38 to help you to a fuller understanding of the text.

36 Now one of the Pharisees invited Jesus to have dinner with him, so he went to the Pharisee's house and reclined at the table. 37 When a woman who had lived a sinful life in that town learned that Jesus was eating at the Pharisee's house, she brought an alabaster jar of perfume, 38 and as she stood behind him at his feet weeping, she began to wet his feet with her tears. Then she wiped them with her hair, kissed them and poured perfume on them.

39 When the Pharisee who had invited him saw this, he said to himself, "If this man were a prophet, he would know who is touching him and what kind of woman she is—that she is a sinner."

⁴⁰ Jesus answered him, "Simon, I have something to tell you."

"Tell me, teacher," he said.

⁴¹ "Two men owed money to a certain moneylender. One owed him five hundred denarii, and the other fifty. ⁴² Neither of them had the money to pay him back, so he canceled the debts of both. Now which of them will love him more?"

⁴³ Simon replied, "I suppose the one who had the bigger debt canceled."

"You have judged correctly," Jesus said.

⁴⁴ Then he turned toward the woman and said to Simon, "Do you see this woman? I came into your house. You did not give me any water for my feet, but she wet my feet with her tears and wiped them with her hair. ⁴⁵ You did not give me a kiss, but this woman, from the time I entered, has not stopped kissing my feet. ⁴⁶ You did not put oil on my head, but she has poured perfume on my feet. ⁴⁷ Therefore, I tell you, her many sins have been forgiven—for she loved much. But he who has been forgiven little loves little."

⁴⁸ Then Jesus said to her, "Your sins are forgiven."

⁴⁹ The other guests began to say among themselves, "Who is this who even forgives sins?"

⁵⁰ Jesus said to the woman, "Your faith has saved you; go in peace."

Luke 7:36–50, NIV

1. If you were to assign a color to this passage, what color would it be?
   ❑ red—because of the tension in the air
   ❑ yellow—because of the warmth expressed by Jesus to the woman
   ❑ blue—because of the coldness of the Pharisees
   ❑ passionate pink—because of the sensual way the woman expressed herself
   ❑ other: _____

2. Why did this "sinful" woman express her repentance and devotion the way she did, instead of expressing herself verbally?
   ❑ she didn't feel worthy to talk to Jesus
   ❑ she was more adept at communicating through touch than through words
   ❑ there were no words to say what she felt
   ❑ she thought Jesus would appreciate the touching more
   ❑ other: _____

3. What surprises you most about Jesus' behavior in this story?
   ❑ that he was eating with a Pharisee in the first place
   ❑ that he would let a sinful woman touch him in such a way
   ❑ that he would forgive this woman just because she kissed his feet
   ❑ that he didn't discourage such groveling behavior (a sign of poor self-image!)
   ❑ none of it surprises me
   ❑ other: _____

"It is a major preoccupation with culture—some would say the occupation of culture—to decide how to organize itself around sexuality."
—Tim Stafford

4. Which two of the following statements reflect your attitude toward human sexuality?
   - ❐ sexuality is an important part of being human
   - ❐ sexuality is overemphasized in our society
   - ❐ sexuality was given by God primarily for enjoyment
   - ❐ sexuality represents a total-person response to another; that is, physically, emotionally, and spiritually
   - ❐ sexuality is "the spice of life"
   - ❐ sexuality is a burden to be endured
   - ❐ sexuality is the response of an individual to a person of the opposite sex
   - ❐ sexuality was given by God primarily for procreation
   - ❐ sexuality is a factor in every one of our relationships

5. If you had been this woman, what would you have done differently?
   - ❐ I would never have entered the Pharisee's home uninvited!
   - ❐ I would have just told Jesus how I felt
   - ❐ I would have thrown the alabaster jar at Simon the Pharisee!
   - ❐ I would have avoided touching Jesus entirely
   - ❐ other: _____

6. Had you been in Jesus' place, how would you have reacted to this woman's behavior?
   - ❐ I probably would have been turned on by it
   - ❐ I would have insisted on washing my feet first
   - ❐ I would have been embarrassed
   - ❐ I would have given her a lecture on positive self-image
   - ❐ I would have cried at experiencing such an act of love

7. What do you think about the kind of affectionate touching this woman showed?
   - ❐ I am embarrassed by it
   - ❐ I desire it, but it should only be for married people
   - ❐ I desire it, and it's OK
   - ❐ it's generally just a prelude to sexual intercourse
   - ❐ I can take it or leave it

8. In what ways should Christian friends (who want to be sexually responsible) show their affection for each other through touching?

9. Most commentators believe that this woman's "sinful life" consisted of sexually immoral behavior and probably prostitution (see the Reference Notes). In light of this, what do you think her first challenge was after Jesus forgave her sins?
   - ❐ how do I support myself financially?
   - ❐ how do I satisfy my sexual needs now?
   - ❐ how do I relate to my former customers?
   - ❐ how do I convince people I've changed?
   - ❐ how do I forgive myself for my past?

LEADER: When you have completed the Bible study, move on to the Caring Time (page 36).

10. What is your biggest challenge or need with respect to your sexuality?
    - ❏ finding the affection I need
    - ❏ satisfying my physical desires
    - ❏ just feeling like a man/woman
    - ❏ putting my past behind me
    - ❏ feeling the security of being held
    - ❏ being affirmed as an attractive person
    - ❏ controlling my impulses
    - ❏ other: _____

COMMENT

An act of extravagance or foolishness? What the woman did to Jesus was an act of love and devotion. The manner in which she chose to display her devotion also allowed her to express her sexuality.

The disciples were probably offended for a number of reasons—beginning with the simple fact that this woman was a known prostitute. In addition, they knew that the perfume could have been sold for a great deal of money and used to help the poor.

But Jesus appreciates her gift and the manner in which she gave it to him. Affirming her and her gift, Jesus affirmed her sexuality. Jesus' actions clarify the distinction between sexuality and sexual activity. We are sexual beings; despite the distortion of our sexuality as single adults by our world (and sometimes by the church), we should celebrate all of who we are. For we are created in God's image.

Learning Control
1 Thessalonians 4:1–8

STUDY

Read 1 Thessalonians 4:1–8 and discuss the questions which follow with your group. Paul's converts were often persons from a Greek background, and the Greek culture of this time had little teaching about sexual morality. Therefore Paul often had to include teaching on this subject in his letters. This is what he does here in his letter to the church at Thessalonica. If you have questions concerning a word or phrase, consult the Reference Notes on page 38.

4 Finally, brothers, we instructed you how to live in order to please God, as in fact you are living. Now we ask you and urge you in the Lord Jesus to do this more and more. ² For you know what instructions we gave you by the authority of the Lord Jesus.

³ It is God's will that you should be sanctified: that you should avoid sexual immorality; ⁴ that each of you should learn to control his own body in a way that is holy and honorable, ⁵ not in passionate lust like the heathen, who do not know God; ⁶ and that in this matter no one should wrong his brother or take advantage of him. The Lord will punish men for all such sins, as we have already told you and warned you. ⁷ For God did not call us to be impure, but to live a holy life. ⁸ Therefore, he who rejects this instruction does not reject man but God, who gives you his Holy Spirit.

1 Thessalonians 4:1–8, NIV

34

1. What's your initial reaction to Paul's teachings?
   - ❏ sounds pretty dogmatic and narrow
   - ❏ that was fine for his time, but we live in a new day
   - ❏ the teaching is good, but the threat of punishment goes too far
   - ❏ this is just what we need in our sexually permissive age
   - ❏ other: _____

2. If you could ask Paul one question to clarify his teaching here, what might it be?
   - ❏ "How can you be sure you speak 'by the authority of the Lord Jesus'?"
   - ❏ "Is all sex outside of marriage included in 'sexual immorality'?"
   - ❏ "Does all sex outside of marriage wrong a brother or sister?"
   - ❏ "Are there some specific techniques I can use to 'learn to control my own body'?"
   - ❏ "Are the punishments you talk about in this life or the next?"
   - ❏ other: _____

3. How would Paul's attitudes toward abstinence and sexual pleasure go over in your workplace?
   - ❏ like a lead balloon
   - ❏ he'd be laughed out of the place
   - ❏ these views would start a lot of arguments
   - ❏ on the surface they would laugh, but deep down they would know he was right
   - ❏ he would be a breath of fresh air

4. Finish this sentence: "To live up to these standards Paul has set, a person would have to..."
   - ❏ be neutered
   - ❏ have a low sex drive
   - ❏ have great personal discipline
   - ❏ have a very close relationship to God
   - ❏ have a group for support and to keep him/her accountable

5. What examples of persons using sex to "wrong a brother or sister or take advantage of him/her" disturb you the most?
   - ❏ date rape
   - ❏ one person doing a disappearing act "the morning after"
   - ❏ making a person a trophy to be bragged about to friends
   - ❏ fading out of the picture when a pregnancy occurs
   - ❏ verbal abuse after a sexual encounter
   - ❏ teasing someone or leading him/her along in regard to sex
   - ❏ a person who lies about his/her marital status
   - ❏ committing adultery
   - ❏ sexual harassment in the workplace
   - ❏ other: _____

"[Sexuality] has to do with—perhaps more than anything else—our capacity for relationships, our desire for connectedness, our longing to be one with somebody, our yearning to transcend our separateness."
—Letha Dawson Scanzoni

6. Which of the following has helped you to control your sexual impulses?
   - ☐ regular devotions and prayer
   - ☐ cold showers
   - ☐ avoiding magazines, movies, or businesses which might play to my passions
   - ☐ getting involved in work or projects as a distraction
   - ☐ the support and encouragement of Christian friends
   - ☐ the cooperation of my "significant other"
   - ☐ nothing seems to work for me
   - ☐ other: _____

7. On the following scale, how much control do you feel you have over your body?

1	2	3	4	5	6	7	8	9	10
About to "crash and burn!"				I'm in a "controlled skid"				In complete control!	

LEADER: When you have completed the Bible study, move on to the Caring Time (below).

8. What are some ways you can express your sexuality without actually having sexual intercourse?

CARING TIME / 20 Minutes / All Together

Leader: Bring all the foursomes back together for a time of caring. Follow the three steps below.

SHARING

Ask group members to finish this sentence:

> *"In light of what I have learned this session, one lifestyle change I need to make is....."*

PRAYER

During your time of prayer, remember the person next to you and what they shared with you. You may say your prayer in silence, ending with a verbal "Amen," so that the next person will know when to start.

ACTION

1. Remember your neighbor's prayer request throughout the week. Drop him/her a note of encouragement with respect to their prayer request.

2. Reflect on the Scripture passages in this study throughout the week—thinking about the difference between sexual activity and sexuality.

REFERENCE NOTES:
LUKE 7:36–50

Summary... The woman's tears show her extreme conviction as she stood by the feet of Jesus. For a woman to loose her hair in public was scandalous. Using it to dry her tears from Jesus' feet marked her great humility before him. Normally, a person's head would be anointed as a sign of honor. Perhaps this woman (like John the Baptist in 3:16) felt she was so unworthy that she could dare only anoint Jesus' feet.

Simon, seeing only that Jesus violated the acceptable religious and social code by allowing such a woman to touch him like this, saw nothing of her repentance or gratitude. If he had invited Jesus to dinner with the hope of finding something to contradict the rumors that Jesus was a great prophet of God, he was sure he had it now. Since Jesus did not draw away from the woman, either he did not know what type of woman she was (showing he lacked a prophet's discernment), or he was not put off by her immorality (showing he lacked a prophet's holiness).

Through a brief parable and interpretation, Jesus disarms Simon's silent criticism. He reveals that he indeed does discern what is in the hearts of people (both with the woman *and* Simon), and that he is concerned about holiness which comes about through the forgiveness of sin. With this parable Jesus highlights his mission of saving those who recognize their sin, and forces Simon (as well as the reader) to question whether he has ever dealt with the reality of his own sin.

While Simon had not behaved discourteously to Jesus as his guest, he hadn't performed any of the special acts of hospitality that were customary for important guests. Barclay notes that, "When a guest entered. . . the host. . . gave him the kiss of peace. . . a mark of respect which was never omitted in the case of a distinguished Rabbi. . . cool water was poured over the guest's feet to cleanse and comfort them. Either a pinch of sweet-smelling incense was burned or a drop of attar of roses was placed on the guest's head." By contrast this woman, who owed nothing to Jesus from a social point of view, showed her love and respect for Jesus by cleansing his feet, welcoming him with her kisses, and anointing him with expensive perfume.

Jesus is not saying that the woman is forgiven *because* she has shown such extravagant love (just as the debt was not cancelled because of any act on the part of the creditor—v. 42), but that her love expresses the reality of the forgiveness she has received. The latter part of the verse is a general statement meant to penetrate Simon's hardness. His coolness and lack of love which is for Jesus shows he has not recognized the enormity of his debt before God, much less his desperate need of forgiveness.

v. 36 **one of the Pharisees**... "The fact that (Jesus) was especially interested in despised people did not mean that he was uninterested in the more respectable members of society" (Marshall). Why Simon (v. 40) invited him is unclear. Since he didn't provide Jesus with some of the common courtesies extended to guests (vv. 44–46), it indicates that he had a low opinion of Jesus. **reclined at the table**... People ate by reclining on their left side on low couches which were arranged around a table (so that their feet would be stretched out behind them).

v. 37 **a sinful life**... Probably a life of sexual immorality is meant. The woman, who was certainly not an invited guest, may simply have joined other people in Simon's courtyard who had gathered to listen to Jesus talk.

vv. 41–43 **five hundred denarii. . . fifty**... The difference here is between owing the equivalent of what one could earn in eighteen months versus owing what could be earned in two months. Then, as now, it would be a rare moneylender who would cancel either debt! Simon rightly gets the point that the man with the greater debt would be more grateful.

v. 48 **Your sins are forgiven**... Jesus confirms that what the woman sensed (and then expressed with her gratitude) was indeed true—she was forgiven of her sin before God.

v. 49 Just as people were assuming Jesus was a prophet (7:29–30, 39), he raises the stakes by claiming divine authority. His audience is shocked by this assertion of divine privilege (see 5:21).

v. 50 **Your faith has saved you...** "Her faith in him and the grace of God. . ." (Geldenhuys). It is trusting oneself to Jesus that leads to salvation (deliverance) from the penalty and power of sin. **Go in peace...** This was a common saying, but, on the lips of Jesus, is uttered not simply as a wish but as an expression of fact. Because she has been forgiven of her sin, peace (with God, herself, and others) is hers to enjoy. By contrast, Simon is left in confusion about his situation.

REFERENCE NOTES:
1 THESSALONIANS
4:1–8

Summary... Paul instructs the Thessalonians to avoid sexual immorality, and to control their bodies. He especially wants them to not "wrong a brother or take advantage of him" in relationship to sexual behavior. He asserts that this is not just his opinion, but God's direction.

v. 1 **live in order to please God...** Just as a spouse desires to please his or her mate, so the Christian's concern is how to please God. Neither is a matter of simply keeping legalistic rules, but involves a lifestyle that reflects an intimate awareness of the other person.

v. 3 **sanctified...** This is to be set apart for God's use. Something that is sanctified ultimately reflects God's character. The emphasis here is that Christians are not to passively wait for God to make them holy, but are to pursue it in dependence upon the Spirit (Rom. 6:13; 8:13). **sexual immorality...** While sanctification is far more than sexual purity, it includes it. This term is an inclusive one for sexual sin—including fornication, adultery, prostitution, and homosexuality. All of these were routine realities in pagan life. New Christians from this environment did not automatically give up these practices, but had to be instructed about the new way in Christ (1 Cor. 5:1–2; 6:9, 12–18).

v. 4 **control his own body...** Lit. "keep (or gain) his own vessel." Although all commentators agree that Paul is using a metaphor here, there is disagreement about what it means! The marginal reading in the NIV represents the alternative view of "learn to acquire a wife." In either case, Paul insists on sexual self-control (in contrast to being controlled by lustful sexual impulses). If the marginal reading is correct, he is saying that sexual activity in marriage is to be carried out in a way that respects the dignity and worth of the woman. This would be a revolutionary idea in a culture that viewed the sexual role of women simply in terms of fulfilling a man's desire.

v. 6 **in this matter no one should wrong his brother...** Adultery or homosexuality within the church itself may be in view here.

vv. 6b–8 The three reasons for sexual purity are: (1) Jesus will punish those who continue in those practices (6b; see also 1 Cor. 9–10); (2) God has called Christians to live a holy life which reflects his nature of faithfulness, integrity, and purity (v. 7); and (3) to reject this teaching is to reject God's Spirit in favor of an unholy way of life (v. 8). The connection of the Holy Spirit with sexual purity is seen also in 1 Corinthians 6:17, 19–20.

SESSION 5

Rejection

PURPOSE: To discover ways to handle rejection, and to accept those who are usually rejected by society.

AGENDA: Gathering Bible Study ♡ Caring Time

GATHERING / 10 Minutes / All Together

Leader: Read the instructions for Step One and go first. Then read the introduction and explain the Bible study choices.

OPEN

Step One: THE STORY OF MY SENIOR PROM. If Hollywood made a movie about your life on the night of your high school prom, what would be needed? Let each person in your group have a few minutes to recall these details. If you didn't go to your Senior Prom, report instead on your "Most Memorable Date." If you have more than 4 or 5 in your group, ask everyone to choose 2 or 3 topics.

1. LOCATION: Where were you living?
2. WEIGHT: How much did you weigh—soaking wet?
3. PROM: Where was it held?
4. DATE: Who did you go with?
5. CAR/TRANSPORTATION: How did you get there?
    (If you used a car, what was the model, year, color, condition?)
6. ATTIRE: What did you wear?
7. PROGRAM: What was the entertainment?
8. AFTERWARD: What did you do afterward?
9. HIGHLIGHT: What was the highlight of the evening?
10. HOMECOMING: If you could go back and visit your high school, who would you like to see?

INTRODUCTION

Step Two: REJECTION. Rejection is one of those unpleasant experiences all of us face from time to time. After all, who hasn't felt left out or rejected at some point in their life? But for some people, rejection is a way of life. For minorities, the poor, the unskilled, and the handicapped, rejection is a familiar companion. Whenever it comes, rejection is painful.

Many singles have experienced rejection—some of us have been divorced; others have had suitors reject us for someone else; still others have never married in the first place (due to experiences of rejection going back to

LEADER: Choose the Track One Bible study (below) or the Track Two study (page 42).

childhood). We cannot avoid such experiences entirely, but we can learn to deal with our feelings about them in better ways. Being rejected by others does not mean we must reject ourselves!

This session will help us look at our experiences of rejection, and how we can improve the way we handle such experiences emotionally. In the Track One study (from Luke's Gospel), we see that Jesus also experienced rejection. We will look at how he handled it, and what that says to us. In the Track Two study (from Peter's first letter), we will consider how being rejected by people is of secondary importance to being accepted and used by God.

BIBLE STUDY / 30 Minutes / Groups of 4

Leader: Help the group decide on Track One or Track Two for their Bible study. Remember to divide into groups of 4 if there are more than 7. Ask one person in each group to be the Convener. Remind the Convener to move the group along so the Bible study can be completed in 30 minutes.

You Can't Go Home Again
Luke 4:14–30

STUDY

Read Luke 4:14–30 and discuss your responses to the following questions with your group. This passage describes an experience of rejection Jesus had when he returned to his hometown shortly after he began his ministry. Check the Reference Notes on pages 45–46 to help you understand the background and some of the difficult phrases in this passage.

> *14 Jesus returned to Galilee in the power of the Spirit, and news about him spread through the whole countryside. 15 He taught in their synagogues, and everyone praised him.*
> *16 He went to Nazareth, where he had been brought up, and on the Sabbath day he went into the synagogue, as was his custom. And he stood up to read. 17 The scroll of the prophet Isaiah was handed to him. Unrolling it, he found the place where it is written:*
>
> > *18 "The Spirit of the Lord is on me,*
> > *because he has anointed me*
> > *to preach good news to the poor.*
> > *He has sent me to proclaim freedom for the prisoners*
> > *and recovery of sight for the blind,*
> > *to release the oppressed,*
> > *19 to proclaim the year of the Lord's favor."*
>
> *20 Then he rolled up the scroll, gave it back to the attendant and sat down. The eyes of everyone in the synagogue were fastened on him, 21 and he began by saying to them, "Today this scripture is fulfilled in your hearing."*
> *22 All spoke well of him and were amazed at the gracious words that came from his lips. "Isn't this Joseph's son?" they asked.*

²³ Jesus said to them, "Surely you will quote this proverb to me: 'Physician, heal yourself! Do here in your hometown what we have heard that you did in Capernaum.'"

²⁴ "I tell you the truth," he continued, "no prophet is accepted in his hometown. ²⁵ I assure you that there were many widows in Israel in Elijah's time, when the sky was shut for three and a half years and there was a severe famine throughout the land. ²⁶ Yet Elijah was not sent to any of them, but to a widow in Zarephath in the region of Sidon. ²⁷ And there were many in Israel with leprosy in the time of Elisha the prophet, yet not one of them was cleansed—only Naaman the Syrian."

²⁸ All the people in the synagogue were furious when they heard this. ²⁹ They got up, drove him out of the town, and took him to the brow of the hill on which the town was built, in order to throw him down the cliff. ³⁰ But he walked right through the crowd and went on his way.

Luke 4:14–30, NIV

1. Why do you think Jesus returned to his hometown of Nazareth?
   ❐ he knew that the people were spiritually lost and needed his message
   ❐ he wanted to show the hometown folks he had "made it"
   ❐ he was fulfilling Old Testament prophecy
   ❐ he was setting up his own rejection

2. When you first went back to your hometown, was your reception similar to Jesus' experience?
   ❐ yes—they were very much alike
   ❐ there were a few similarities
   ❐ no—I was welcomed to my hometown
   ❐ I haven't left my hometown

3. What do you like best about your childhood hometown? What do you like least? Would you ever want to go back there to live? Why or why not?

4. How would you describe Jesus' attitude toward the Nazarenes?
   ❐ he cared about them, but he knew that they would reject him
   ❐ he had "a chip on his shoulder" toward them
   ❐ he was apathetic toward them
   ❐ he wanted them to hear the truth and accept it
   ❐ he disdained them

5. Why did Jesus refuse to perform a miracle to convince them that he was the Messiah?
   ❐ he was tired of having to perform for others
   ❐ he wanted them to accept him based on what they had heard
   ❐ he wanted them to accept him just as he was
   ❐ he wanted them to believe by faith and not by sight
   ❐ he knew they wouldn't believe in him even if he performed miracles

6. How was Jesus affected when he was rejected by his hometown?
   ❐ he was upset
   ❐ he anticipated rejection and wasn't particularly bothered by it
   ❐ he wasn't affected by the rejection at all
   ❐ he was scared and shaken
   ❐ he was hurt, but didn't show it

"Rejection occurs when love is withdrawn, knowingly or unknowingly, and when a person is denied the right or opportunity to be or become a person."
—Charles R. Solomon

7. Which of the following best describes how you react to rejection?
   ❒ I laugh it off
   ❒ I stew about it for days
   ❒ I make sure I reject them as well
   ❒ I examine myself to find how I can improve
   ❒ I go to a friend for reassurance
   ❒ I go to God for a little "self-worth repair"
   ❒ I don't remember ever being rejected
   ❒ other: _____

8. Which of the following experiences of rejection have you gone through? Which one was hardest for you?
   ❒ not being wanted when I was born
   ❒ being adopted from my natural family
   ❒ being rejected for adoptions
   ❒ having a parent abandon me
   ❒ having someone I loved leave me for someone else
   ❒ being fired
   ❒ being divorced
   ❒ being rejected because of my race
   ❒ being rejected because of my physical disability

LEADER: When you have completed the Bible study, move on to the Caring Time (page 44).

9. What do you feel you need to do about your past rejections?
   ❒ forget them
   ❒ talk to someone about them
   ❒ talk to the ones who rejected me
   ❒ pray about them
   ❒ learn from them

COMMENT

No one likes rejection. We all want to be loved and accepted for who we are. It can be tough to handle rejection when it comes our way, but it is much more difficult for us to deal with rejection from those closest to us. If we yearn for anyone's approval, we want it from those who have known us the longest.

Jesus faced rejection from those in his hometown. They had heard so much about him. His reputation for healing and teaching preceded him. But they could not believe that he was who he said he was. After all, this was Mary and Joseph's son. They remembered Jesus as a little boy, running around town with their kids. Jesus no longer fit their view. This was unfortunate, because the people of Nazareth missed out on quite a bit.

Rejected by Men
1 Peter 2:4–10

STUDY

Read 1 Peter 2:4–10 and discuss your responses to the following questions with your group. In this passage, we are told that even though people rejected Jesus, God used him in a very important way. If you have trouble with a word or phrase, check the Reference Notes on pages 46–47.

⁴ As you come to him, the living Stone—rejected by men but chosen by God and precious to him— ⁵ you also, like living stones, are being built into a spiritual house to be a holy priesthood, offering spiritual sacrifices acceptable to God through Jesus Christ. ⁶ For in Scripture it says:

> *"See, I lay a stone in Zion,*
> *a chosen and precious cornerstone,*
> *and the one who trusts in him*
> *will never be put to shame."*

⁷ Now to you who believe, this stone is precious. But to those who do not believe,

> *"The stone the builders rejected*
> *has become the capstone,"*

⁸ and,

> *"A stone that causes men to stumble*
> *and a rock that makes them fall."*

They stumble because they disobey the message—which is also what they were destined for.
⁹ But you are a chosen people, a royal priesthood, a holy nation, a people belonging to God, that you may declare the praises of him who called you out of darkness into his wonderful light. ¹⁰ Once you were not a people, but now you are the people of God; once you had not received mercy, but now you have received mercy.

1 Peter 2:4–10, NIV

1. If you didn't know who had written this and you had to draw a picture of what you think the person looked like, what picture would you draw?
   - ❏ a construction worker with a hard hat on
   - ❏ a starry-eyed poet reciting his work
   - ❏ a preacher in a pulpit
   - ❏ a desert prophet

2. What do you think is the most important contrast in this passage?
   - ❏ between being rejected by people and chosen by God
   - ❏ between what people may once have been, and what they are
   - ❏ between how believers see Christ and how nonbelievers see him

3. Why is Peter writing to these people about Jesus' rejection?
   - ❏ so they can get back at those who rejected him
   - ❏ to warn them against rejecting him as well
   - ❏ to help them put their own rejection in perspective
   - ❏ to help them see the difference between God's perspective and people's perspective

4. When do you first remember feeling that your "stone" (your contribution to what was being done or built) was being rejected?
   - ❏ when my parents wouldn't let me help out when I was a child
   - ❏ when as a child, I was cut from a sports team or musical group
   - ❏ when as a youth, my church wouldn't let me take a role in worship
   - ❏ when I was fired from a part-time job
   - ❏ when I was rejected by someone I had a childhood crush on
   - ❏ other: _____

"Acceptance of a person requires a tolerance of imperfection."
—Robert K. Greenleaf

43

5. When did you last feel that your "stone" was being rejected?

6. What is the most important thing this passage says to you about your experiences of rejection?
   - ❐ God has the last say on who is rejected or accepted (v. 4)
   - ❐ God has an important role for me in what he is doing (v. 5)
   - ❐ if people rejected Jesus, shouldn't I expect the same? (vv. 7–8)
   - ❐ whoever else rejects me, I will always belong with God (v. 9)
   - ❐ my identity is in God, not in how well I please people (vv. 9–10)

7. How have you "received mercy" from God in the times of rejection you have experienced?

8. How does your status with God affect the way you relate to people who have rejected you in the past?
   - ❐ I can tell them "Nyah!—Nyah!—Nyah!"
   - ❐ I don't have to hate them, because God has rescued me from the pain
   - ❐ I can feel sorry for them because of their rejection by God
   - ❐ I can return good for evil, because I am God's
   - ❐ it doesn't affect it, because I'm still too angry
   - ❐ it gives me the desire to help them turn to God for rescue from their rejection

LEADER: When you have completed the Bible study, move on to the Caring Time (below).

CARING TIME / 20 Minutes / All Together

Leader: Bring all the foursomes back together for a time of caring. Follow the three steps below. Be sensitive to the sharing about rejection.

SHARING

Ask each person in the group to share: Who will you see in the coming week that has rejected you in the past? What help do you need to deal with that relationship?

PRAYER

During your time of prayer, remember the people who shared and what they said. Remembering the requests which were just shared, close with a prayer time. The Leader can start a conversational prayer (short phrases and sentences), with group members following. After an appropriate amount of time, the Leader can close by praying for any requests not already mentioned. Remember people in your church and community who might feel rejected.

ACTION

1. Think of someone who feels on the "outside"—not accepted by your church or community. This may be an older person or a person with a different background than yours.

2. Make a plan to make them feel more accepted or included. For example, visit someone in a nursing home, invite the person to a fellowship time at your church, or invite the person to your home for lunch.

3. This coming week send a card, write a note of encouragement, or phone someone you know who is going through a difficult time, and encourage them in the faith.

**REFERENCE NOTES:
LUKE 4:14–30**

Summary... As this passage shows, the response to Jesus' ministry was mixed. On the one hand, his ministry was highly popular with the crowds. This was to be expected in a day of little (and reliable) medical care (Jesus effectively healed a variety of diseases). These were days in which little could be done about demon possession (Jesus effectively cast out all sorts of demons). It was also a time when the rabbinic teaching was pedantic and boring (while Jesus was praised as a powerful teacher). On the other hand, he was opposed by the people in his own hometown (who scorned him as one who pretended—in their view—to be someone he could not possibly be) and the religious leaders (who feared Jesus because he did not follow their ways).

v. 14 **Galilee**... In 4:14–9:50, Luke records Jesus' ministry in Galilee, a province fifty miles long and twenty-five miles wide in the north of Palestine. **in the power of the Spirit**... Just as the Spirit led Jesus into his time of testing (Mt. 4:1; Lk. 4:1), so the Spirit now empowers Jesus' ministry.

v. 15 **synagogues**... While the Temple in Jerusalem was the religious center for all Jews, the community synagogue was the focal point of weekly worship and teaching. Jesus has taught in synagogues throughout Galilee. He comes to his hometown of Nazareth in light of the stories of his healings and teachings.

vv. 16–30 Luke uses this scene to introduce crucial themes of Jesus' ministry: (1) The nature of Jesus' mission in proclaiming that he is the agent through which God's people will be delivered (vv. 18–21); (2) The rejection Jesus will receive from many (vv. 28–29); and (3) The fact that the message of the kingdom of God is not restricted to Israel, but is for all people (vv. 24–27).

v. 16 **Nazareth**... Nazareth, a town of about twenty thousand people, was located in a hollow surrounded by hills. **the Sabbath**... Each Sabbath, Jews would gather at the synagogue for a service of worship and instruction from the Scripture. There was a standard order of passages from the Law which were read. The synagogue had no formal clergy. So various men (who were approved by the elders of the synagogue) read and taught the Scripture. Given Jesus' emerging reputation, it is not surprising that he was asked to read and teach. **he stood up to read**... This was a sign of reverence for God. But rabbis would sit down to teach (v. 20). **the scroll**... Since Nazareth was a small village, it is unlikely that the synagogue could have afforded scrolls of all OT writings. The Isaiah scroll was undoubtedly a prized possession.

v. 18 The passage Jesus read was from Isaiah 61:1–2 (with the addition of a phrase from 58:6). Using the metaphors of people in prison, blindness, and slavery, the prophet speaks of his God-given mission to proclaim freedom and pardon to people who are oppressed and burdened. **The Spirit of the Lord is upon me**... The ministry of a prophet of God is empowered by God's Spirit. **to preach good news/to proclaim freedom/recovery of sight**... In the context of the Isaiah passage, this meant that God was going to deliver the Jews from their captivity in Babylon. **release the oppressed**... These words are not found in either the Hebrew or Greek versions of Isaiah 61, but may be a commentary on the meaning of the "recovery of sight" (borrowed from a phrase in Isaiah 58:6).

v. 19 **the year of the Lord's favor**... This specifically refers to the Jubilee Year of Leviticus 25. Every fifty years, the Jews were to release their slaves, cancel all debts, and return land to the families of its original owners.

v. 21 **Today this Scripture is fulfilled**… Jesus asserts that the new era which was foretold by Isaiah has begun. Isaiah's language regarding restored sight and release from slavery was figurative. Jesus' healings and exorcisms pointed to the truth that the new era of God's deliverance had begun, and would come to pass through him. He is the one who truly does give sight.

v. 22 **All spoke well of him**… The Greek word *martureo* (here translated in the positive sense) can also be translated "to condemn" or "to speak against" (compare Ac. 13:22 with Mt. 23:31). The violent response later in this story (v. 28) shows that the final reaction toward Jesus was decidedly negative. Despite an initially positive reaction, the congregation is quickly shocked at the way Jesus applies this passage to himself. **amazed**… Likewise, this word can express admiration (7:9) or opposition.

v. 23 **Physician, heal yourself**… The proverb has both Greek and Arabic parallels. The doubt and cynicism of his hometown is seen in that they would not believe the stories they had heard elsewhere, unless they could see further evidence. **Capernaum**… According to Mark, this is the village where Jesus first began to teach and heal (Mk. 1:21ff).

v. 24 **no prophet is accepted in his hometown**… This proverb observes that the hardest place for a famous person to gain respect is among the people he or she grew up with. The irony is that while they will honor Isaiah as a prophet, they refuse to see the fulfillment of his prophecy in Jesus.

vv. 25–29 While neither Elijah nor Elisha were rejected by their own people, their ministry extended to others outside of Israel as well. These stories (found in 1 Kings 17:1–18:1 and 2 Kings 5:1–27) illustrate that God has never confined his grace to Israel alone. They further emphasize the point that if Nazareth (and, by extension, all Jews) will not receive Jesus with faith, then there are plenty of others (including Gentiles) who will. This was inflammatory language! Jesus' strong words implied that Gentiles were more worthy of God's grace than the people from Jesus' hometown. This provoked such a strong response that a mob desired to kill him.

Summary… Peter tells his readers that Jesus may have been rejected by people, but he is the one God will use as the "capstone" of his new kingdom. In the building of that kingdom, each believer is like a living stone which contributes to the whole. Changing images, he says that believers (even those who before had been Gentiles and who had no unity among them, are now brought together as one people, chosen by God to bring others to him.

**REFERENCE NOTES:
1 PETER 2:4–10**

v. 4 **come to him**… This phrase "expresses the idea of drawing near with intention both to stay and to enjoy personal fellowship" (Stibbs). **the living Stone**… Peter gets this metaphor from Isaiah 28:16 (v. 6) and Psalm 118:22 (v. 7). Peter's point is that despite his rejection by the world, Christ is the chosen one of God who is alive and able to give his resurrection life to those who come to him. The implication is that Jesus' experience should assure these Christians that despite the hard times they are facing, like Christ they will also come through it all to a glorious future. **precious**… People may reject Jesus, but God gives him great honor. The word "precious" means "prized" or "highly esteemed."

46

v. 5 **you also, like living stones**... So close is the relationship between Christians and Christ that Peter uses the same metaphor to describe both. The implication is that these Christians, like Christ, will know both rejection and triumph. **being built into**... Stones by themselves, lying around on the ground, serve little function. But shaped together into a structure by a master builder, they become useful and important. **a spiritual house**... As living stones, they have been built into a holy temple in which God dwells (see also Mk. 14:58; 1 Cor. 3:9–17; 2 Cor. 6:16; Eph. 2:20–22; Heb. 3:2–6). **a holy priesthood**... Not only are they a "spiritual house," they are the priests who serve in it! Typically, priests were privileged and set apart. But no such elitism exists in the Church. All Christians are members of this royal priesthood. **spiritual sacrifices**... Priests offered material sacrifices of animals, grain, and wine. The sacrifice of Christians, however, consists of spiritual qualities like love, faith, surrender, service, prayer, thanksgiving, and sharing. (Rom. 12:1; Eph. 5:1–2; Php. 4:18; Heb. 13:15–16). Their sacrifice is also inspired by the Spirit. **acceptable to God through Jesus Christ**... All of their efforts, however, would fail to satisfy God were it not for the sacrifice already made by Jesus himself.

v. 6 In its original context, Isaiah 28:16 referred to the leaders of Israel who had just made a pact with Egypt (in response to the threat of an invasion by Assyria). Isaiah points to the Temple as an illustration of where their true strength lies. They need to trust God, not alliances. Later on, rabbis understood this reference to the cornerstone to be a description of the Messiah whom God would establish in Zion.

v. 7 In its original context, the stone in Psalm 118:22 stood for Israel (which the world powers considered useless and threw away). However, God gave Israel the most important place in building his kingdom. This text was taken by the early church to be a prophecy of Jesus' rejection and subsequent vindication by God (Mk. 12:10; Ac. 4:8–12).

v. 8 In its original context, Isaiah 8:14 referred to God as the rock over which Israel stumbled (because they refused to follow him).

vv. 9–10 Peter lists a series of titles (drawn primarily from Isaiah 43:20–21 and Exodus 19:5–6) to describe the destiny which belongs to Christians. **a chosen people**... Just as Jesus is "chosen by God" (2:4), so are they as his people (see also 1:1–2). **a holy nation**... The Church is not holy "in the sense that either it or its members are in actual fact paragons of virtue, but because it has been set apart for God's service and is inspired and sustained by His Spirit" (Kelly). **that you may declare the praises of him**... Their role is to make God known in the world. Peter contrasts what they have become with what they once were. This time he draws his language from Hosea 1:6, 9; 2:25.

SESSION 6

Loneliness

PURPOSE: To learn creative ways to move from loneliness to aloneness.

AGENDA: ⬛ Gathering ⬛ Bible Study ♡ Caring Time

GATHERING / 10 Minutes / All Together

Leader: Loneliness is a common feeling for singles, but not one that is openly discussed. So continue to be sensitive to all who share. By this time, group members should feel comfortable enough with each other to share at a deeper level. Read the instructions for Step One and go first. Then read the Introduction and explain the choices for Bible study.

OPEN

Step One: FANTASY TRIP. Answer 3 or 4 of the questions below. Share your answers with the group. If you could plan your fantasy trip...

- ☐ Where would you go? _____
- ☐ Who would you invite along? _____
- ☐ How would you travel? _____
- ☐ What book would you read on your trip? _____
- ☐ If you could take a side trip, where would it be? _____
- ☐ How would you spend most of your time? _____
- ☐ At night, what special things would you do? _____
- ☐ While you're away, what in your life would you like to reevaluate? _____
- _____
- ☐ Before you returned, what letter would you write? _____

INTRODUCTION

Step Two: LONELINESS. Some authorities believe that an epidemic of loneliness is sweeping America. They believe that 1 out of every 2 Americans is lonely. A national study conducted by *Psychology Today* found that 50% of the 40,000 people surveyed reported they sometimes (or often) felt lonely.

One reason offered for this is the fragmentation of family networks. Families are more geographically scattered than in the past, thereby making companionship, support, and comfort less available. Another reason for loneliness is the prevalence of divorce, which often creates isolation from friends. Singles are often lonely as they search for the appropriate person with whom to share their life. While they may have many friends, that one "special friend" is missing.

Nevertheless, loneliness need not be a problem inherent to the single life. There is a difference between "aloneness" and "loneliness." A person can feel lonely in a crowd, because he or she feels no emotional connections to anybody nearby. A person can feel lonely in a marriage, because communication and caring has broken down. In contrast, a person who lives alone may feel the bonds of love and connection with many different people, and hence not be lonely. It is also important for us to note that not all loneliness is bad. Times of loneliness may give a person time for some soul-searching that ends in constructive life changes.

LEADER: Choose the Track One Bible study (below) or the Track Two study (page 51).

What is the purpose of loneliness, and how do we deal with it? That is the question we will face in this session. As we will see in Track One (from Matthew's Gospel), Jesus was familiar with loneliness. The loneliness that he experienced was at its most intense level just before he died. The Apostle Paul also knew loneliness, and it was reflected in his second letter to Timothy (Track Two study). We can learn much from the way they both handled loneliness.

BIBLE STUDY / 30 Minutes / Groups of 4

Leader: Help the group choose a track for study. Divide into groups of 4 for discussion. Remind the Convener for each group to move the group along so the Bible Study can be completed in the time allotted. Have everyone return together for the Caring Time for the final 20 minutes.

Loneliness vs. Aloneness
Matthew 26:36–46

STUDY

Two themes dominate this passage: Jesus' continued obedience to God despite his dread of what was coming, and the disciples' continued failure to grasp what was ahead for Jesus. Read Matthew 26:36–46 and discuss your responses to the following questions with your group. Refer to the Reference Notes on pages 54–55 for further clarification on parts of this passage.

36 Then Jesus went with his disciples to a place called Gethsemane, and he said to them, "Sit here while I go over there and pray." 37 He took Peter and the two sons of Zebedee along with him, and he began to be sorrowful and troubled. 38 Then he said to them, "My soul is overwhelmed with sorrow to the point of death. Stay here and keep watch with me."
39 Going a little farther, he fell with his face to the ground and prayed, "My Father, if it is possible, may this cup be taken from me. Yet not as I will, but as you will."
40 Then he returned to his disciples and found them sleeping. "Could you men not keep watch with me for one hour?" he asked Peter. 41 "Watch and pray so that you will not fall into temptation. The spirit is willing, but the body is weak."
42 He went away a second time and prayed, "My Father, if it is not possible for this cup to be taken away unless I drink it, may your will be done."
43 When he came back, he again found them sleeping, because their eyes were heavy. 44 So he left them and went away once more and prayed the third time, saying the same thing.

45 Then he returned to the disciples and said to them, "Are you still sleeping and resting? Look, the hour is near, and the Son of Man is betrayed into the hands of sinners. 46 Rise, let us go! Here comes my betrayer!"

Matthew 26:36–46, NIV

1. If Jesus could have sung a modern (or relatively modern) song to express how he felt by the end of this story, what song do you think he might have sung?
   ❑ "I Ain't Got Nobody"
   ❑ "Yesterday (All my troubles seemed so far away)"—the Beatles
   ❑ "Heal the World"—Michael Jackson
   ❑ "The Impossible Dream"—from *Man of La Mancha*
   ❑ "You'll Never Walk Alone"
   ❑ other: _____

2. Why did Jesus take the disciples with him to Gethsemane?
   ❑ he was distressed and didn't want to be alone
   ❑ he wanted to teach the disciples something
   ❑ he wanted emotional support
   ❑ he realized there was power in numbers
   ❑ he wanted them to stand guard
   ❑ he needed some eyewitnesses to write about it all later

> *"People are lonely because they build walls instead of bridges."*
> *—Joseph F. Newton*

3. How do you think Jesus felt when he said, "Could you men not keep watch with me for one hour?"
   ❑ lonely   ❑ unimportant
   ❑ sympathetic   ❑ angry
   ❑ disappointed   ❑ sad

4. If you had been Jesus, what would you have done if you had come back and found that your "support group" was asleep?
   ❑ poured cold water on them
   ❑ cried
   ❑ left quietly so they could sleep
   ❑ figured I didn't deserve any better
   ❑ yelled at them
   ❑ felt sorry for myself
   ❑ other: _____

5. In your opinion, which of the following pairs of contrasting phrases defines the difference between being lonely and being alone?
   ❑ "forced on me" versus "chosen by me"
   ❑ "an empty cup" versus "filling my bucket"
   ❑ "outwardly focused" versus "inwardly focused"
   ❑ "in despair" versus "at peace"
   ❑ "looking for people" versus "looking for God"
   ❑ "self-pitying" versus "self-exploring"

6. When Jesus went back the third time to pray, was it an experience of loneliness or being alone?

7. Where is your favorite place to go for a time of being alone?
   - ☐ my house or apartment
   - ☐ my room with the door locked
   - ☐ a place on a lake
   - ☐ a motel where nobody knows I am there
   - ☐ in my car on an open highway
   - ☐ a place in the mountains
   - ☐ in a boat
   - ☐ an island hideaway
   - ☐ other: _____

8. If you had to choose three people (not in this group) to be with you in a "Gethsemane experience," who would you choose (and why)?

9. What is the closest you have come to going through a time of stress and soul-searching like Jesus went through in Gethsemane?

LEADER: When you have completed the Bible study, move on to the Caring Time (page 54).

10. In your time of stress, how much were you able to depend on your friends? Use the following scale:

1	2	3	4	5	6	7	8	9	10
They enlisted with the "opposition"			They fell asleep on me			Partially			Completely!

COMMENT

Loneliness. Even the word can cast a shadow over one's day. No one likes to feel lonely. There is comfort in our loneliness in knowing that Jesus experienced such feelings himself. He knew what was ahead for him, and he wanted there to be some other way. At least he had his three closest friends with him. But even they fell asleep and couldn't provide him with the support he needed. So Jesus poured out his soul to God. He prayed. He cried. He felt alone. In the midst of all of his pain, Jesus knew that God was with him. That knowledge eased some of his pain that night, even though his circumstances remained unchanged. And so it is for us in our lonely times as well.

Track 2

Oh, Lonesome Me
2 Timothy 4:9–22

STUDY

Paul concludes this letter to Timothy with a series of personal remarks. He includes comments about mutual acquaintances, information about what has happened to him, and requests for assistance. Read 2 Timothy 4:9–22 and share your responses to the following questions with your group. If you do not understand a particular word or phrase, check the Reference Notes on pages 55–56.

⁹Do your best to come to me quickly, ¹⁰for Demas, because he loved this world, has deserted me and has gone to Thessalonica. Crescens has gone to Galatia, and Titus to Dalmatia. ¹¹Only Luke is with me. Get Mark and bring him with you, because he is helpful to me in my ministry. ¹²I sent Tychicus to Ephesus. ¹³When you come, bring the cloak that I left with Carpus at Troas, and my scrolls, especially the parchments.

14 *Alexander the metalworker did me a great deal of harm. The Lord will repay him for what he has done.* 15 *You too should be on your guard against him, because he strongly opposed our message.*

16 *At my first defense, no one came to my support, but everyone deserted me. May it not be held against them.* 17 *But the Lord stood at my side and gave me strength, so that through me the message might be fully proclaimed and all the Gentiles might hear it. And I was delivered from the lion's mouth.* 18 *The Lord will rescue me from every evil attack and will bring me safely to his heavenly kingdom. To him be glory for ever and ever. Amen.*

19 *Greet Priscilla and Aquila and the household of Onesiphorus.* 20 *Erastus stayed in Corinth, and I left Trophimus sick in Miletus.* 21 *Do your best to get here before winter. Eubulus greets you, and so do Pudens, Linus, Claudia and all the brothers.*

22 *The Lord be with your spirit. Grace be with you.*

2 Timothy 4:9–22, NIV

1. Which of the following words best describe Paul's mood in this passage?
   - ❏ self-pitying
   - ❏ angry
   - ❏ forgiving
   - ❏ paranoid
   - ❏ demanding
   - ❏ lonely
   - ❏ hopeful
   - ❏ bitter
   - ❏ needy
   - ❏ protective

2. If you had been Paul and your friends all deserted you except for one, what would you have done?
   - ❏ gone into self-pity
   - ❏ figured I deserved it
   - ❏ written them all nasty letters
   - ❏ like Paul—depend on God
   - ❏ like Paul—complain to someone else
   - ❏ thanked God for the one friend who stayed
   - ❏ other: _____

3. What "Luke" have you known who stayed with you when others turned away?

4. What is the difference between being lonely and being alone? Which was Paul in this passage?

5. What is your view of loneliness and the single lifestyle?
   - ❏ single people are no more lonely than married people
   - ❏ most singles experience aloneness, but not loneliness
   - ❏ if a person is lonely, it is his/her own fault
   - ❏ loneliness is a state of mind, and not a state of being
   - ❏ other: _____

"It is easy to be lonely, but it is difficult to be alone."
—Paul Tillich

6. Which of the following experiences of loneliness have you had in the last month?
   - ☐ feeling alone in a crowd
   - ☐ feeling abandoned by friends
   - ☐ feeling desperate for a spouse
   - ☐ feeling nobody understood me
   - ☐ feeling everyone was out to get me
   - ☐ having no one to share my pain with
   - ☐ having no one to share my joys with
   - ☐ having no one just to have fun with

7. When in your life have you experienced loneliness so intense that coming out of it was like "being delivered from the lion's mouth" (v. 17)?

8. Which of the following experiences of quiet aloneness have you had in the past month?
   - ☐ feeling perfectly at ease while I was alone
   - ☐ feeling the Lord was at my side, giving me strength (like Paul!)
   - ☐ feeling God was speaking to me
   - ☐ feeling at one with God's creation

LEADER: When you have completed the Bible study, move on to the Caring Time (page 54).

9. How do those times of quiet aloneness help you when times of loneliness come?

10. If you could spend an evening with Paul in his situation now, what could you share from your life story that might encourage him?

COMMENT

Paul begins this final chatty section of his letter with his main request. He wants Timothy to leave his post at Ephesus and join him in Rome. It would not be an easy journey (nor a particularly quick one, given travel conditions). Then Paul explains the reason why he wants Timothy to come: all of his colleagues have left him, except for Luke.

Demas left because he fell in love with the world, and now stands in opposition to God. Crescens and Titus left because of ministry needs. Paul wants Timothy to bring Mark (which indicates that Paul and Mark have reconciled since their blowup). Paul felt betrayed by Alexander, who may have informed against Paul.

Paul then describes his loneliness during his first trial, when no one came to support him. Amid his feelings of being deserted and abandoned, Paul recounts his dependence on the Lord. With no one else there, the Lord stood by Paul's side and gave him strength.

These are encouraging words for all of us in our times of loneliness and despair. Paul's example reminds us that feelings of loneliness come to all— even devout apostles. But the Lord is standing by our side as well.

CARING TIME / 20 Minutes / All Together

Leader: Continue to encourage the group to share openly. At this time in our studies, people should feel more comfortable in their depth of sharing.

SHARING

From the following list, share with the group what you will need most to combat loneliness in the weeks to come:

- ☐ someone to spend time with
- ☐ someone to pray with
- ☐ a new attitude toward aloneness
- ☐ a closer relationship with God
- ☐ a new focus on others
- ☐ a special "Luke" to lean on
- ☐ other: _____

PRAYER

If someone is uncomfortable praying aloud, encourage them to pray silently. When they conclude their prayer, ask them to say "Amen" so the next person will know to continue.

ACTION

1. Plan one thing you can do this week to move from feelings of loneliness to aloneness.

2. Knowing what helps you not to feel lonely, plan to do something this week for someone you know who may be lonely.

REFERENCE NOTES: MATTHEW: 26:36–46

v. 36 **Gethsemane**... This was an olive orchard on an estate at the foot of the Mount of Olives (just outside the eastern wall of Jerusalem). The name literally means "an oil press" (for making olive oil).

v. 39 **prayed**... He prayed aloud, as was customary for people at the time, so the disciples heard (and remembered) his prayer. **My Father**... This was not a title for God that was used in prayer in the first century. It expressed an intimacy that was considered inappropriate. **this cup**... In the OT, drinking a cup of bitter wine was often used as a symbol for experiencing God's judgment (e.g., Ps. 75:8; Isa. 51:17–22). By using this image, Jesus refers to the events of his death which are rapidly approaching. **Yet not as I will, but as you will**... Today, this phrase is popularly used as a generalized "escape clause" when people are unsure what to pray. For Jesus it is actually an affirmation of his intent to pursue the Father's will, even when he did not like it. While he pleads that there might be another way, this sentence declares his commitment to follow the Father's lead, regardless of the cost (see also v. 42).

v. 40 **sleeping**... Although the disciples had vowed never to abandon Jesus (v. 35), these three could not even keep themselves awake to be with him. The issue was not simply that the disciples failed to pray for Jesus in his time of greatest need. It is related to the custom that Passover officially ended when the participants were overcome by sleep. Their falling asleep meant that Passover was over, and God's deliverance of his people had not occurred. In short, there was no hope of divine intervention that would enable Jesus to avoid the cross.

v. 41 To **"watch"** means to "be spiritually alert," lest they fall into the "temptation" to be unfaithful to God. **The spirit/the body**... Probably as in Psalm 51:12, the "spirit" here is the human spirit energized by God. The problem is that the disciples allowed their physical condition to dictate their response to an impending spiritual crisis.

v. 45 **the hour is near**... This is the time of Jesus' death. **into the hands of sinners**... Jesus uses the term to refer to the religious authorities who are on their way to arrest him.

**REFERENCE NOTES:
2 TIMOTHY 4:9–22**

v. 9 **come to me quickly**... Rome was over 1,000 miles from Ephesus. Still, with the typical delays in the Roman judicial system, Paul believes that if Timothy hurries (and gets on a boat before the shipping closes down for winter—v. 21), he will reach Rome before Paul's trial.

v. 10 **Demas**... Apparently, he was a co-worker with Paul during Paul's earlier imprisonment. Therefore, it must have been particularly painful when Demas deserted him. **he loved this world**... The "world" is the system that stands in opposition to God. **deserted**... This is the same word that is used by Jesus on the cross: "My God, my God, why have you forsaken [or "deserted"] me?" **Crescens**... This is the only mention of him in the New Testament. **Titus to Dalmatia**... In Titus 3:12, Paul asks Titus to come to him at Nicopolis. Nicopolis was a city located several hundred miles down the coast from Dalmatia, so perhaps Titus went up to Dalmatia from Nicopolis. Both Titus and Crescens were involved in missionary activity.

v. 11 **Luke**... Luke, a frequent traveling companion, had been with Paul during his earlier imprisonment (Col. 4:14; Philem. 24). Perhaps he stayed on because Paul needed medical attention. **Get Mark and bring him with you**... Mark deserted them in Perga on their first missionary journey (Acts 13:13; 15:36–41), which resulted in the split-up of Paul and Barnabas. Mark is now once again a valued co-worker with Paul (Col. 4:10; Philem. 24).

v. 12 Tychicus is probably the bearer of this letter (see Eph. 6:21–22; Col. 4:7; Titus 3:12). It is quite possible that Paul has sent him to take over Timothy's duties in Ephesus, thus freeing Timothy to come to Rome. Tychicus' departure is the reason Paul needs Mark.

v. 13 **cloak**... This was a heavy wool cape that was worn in the cold and rain. It consisted of a single piece of material with a hole in the middle for the head. Winter was coming, and Paul needed his cloak to stay warm in jail. **scrolls/parchments**... It cannot be known what these contained. Possibilities include: portions of the Old Testament, a Greek Old Testament, blank writing materials, early copies of the Gospels, or official documents (such as Paul's birth certificate).

v. 14 **Alexander**... Two other Alexanders are mentioned in the New Testament. There is the Alexander who, along with Hymenaeus, was excommunicated by Paul (1 Tim. 1:19–20), and Alexander the Jew, who tried to quell the riot in Ephesus (Acts 19:33-34). The Alexander mentioned here might be one of these men, or an otherwise unknown person, since it was a very common name. In any event, this Alexander "strongly opposed" the gospel message (v. 15), and may well have been the one who had Paul arrested and thrown back in jail. **did me a great deal of harm**... The verb here was used to mean "inform against." **The Lord will repay him**... One day Alexander will reap the reward of his act.

v. 16 **At my first defense**... Paul is probably referring to his preliminary hearing before the emperor or a judge. His actual trial would take place at a later date. (During his first imprisonment, there was a two-year gap between his hearing and his trial. See Acts 24:1, 23, 27; 28:16, 30.) **no one came to my support**... This may simply mean that he had no lawyer to defend him. Or it could mean that due to the seriousness of the charge, his friends did not want to risk being identified with him. In any case, Paul felt all alone—"deserted." **May it not be held against them**... This echoes Jesus' words from the cross (Luke 23:34; see also v. 10).

v. 17 **the Lord stood at my side**... This is not the language of religious mysticism. It is the language of someone who has personally encountered the living Christ: a person who is "in him" and who has had his own life invaded by the power of the Holy Spirit. It would have been as natural as breathing for Paul to experience the presence of the Lord at such a time (Fee). **gave me strength**... This is the first of two things the Lord did for Paul at his hearing. The Lord enabled him to proclaim the gospel during the hearing (as he had done during his previous arrest—see Acts 24:1–21). **delivered**... This is the second thing the Lord did for him. Paul was not sentenced to die at this hearing. **from the lion's mouth**... There has been much debate as to who the "lion" might be. Candidates have included Nero, Satan, the Roman Empire, as well as the actual lions in the Coliseum. Given the context here and in the Psalm he is alluding to (Ps. 22:19–21), Paul is probably referring to death. It's his way of saying that he survived his preliminary hearing. The judge was not able to render a verdict; therefore, a full trial was required.

v. 18 Though his enemies may kill his body, evil will never separate him from God's kingdom.

v. 19 **Priscilla and Aquila**... These are old friends whom Paul first met in Corinth. Priscilla apparently played an important part in ministry. Four of the six times she and Aquila appear in the New Testament, her name is mentioned first. It was very unusual in the first century for a woman to be listed before her husband.

v. 21 **Linus**... According to Irenaeus, Linus was the first appointed bishop of Rome following the martyrdom of Paul and Peter.

SESSION 7

Tomorrow

PURPOSE: To anticipate an exciting future.

AGENDA: ☕ Gathering   📖 Bible Study   ♡ Caring Time

GATHERING / 10 Minutes / All Together

Leader: This is the final session together. You may want to have your Caring Time first. If not, be sure to allow a full 25 minutes at the end of the session. Read the instructions for Step One and set the pace by going first. Then read the Introduction and move on to the Bible study.

OPEN

Step One: FUTURE FANTASY. Imagine you have just been given the ability to transport yourself into the future, ten years from now! You step out of the time machine and discover that your life is just as you had hoped it would be. Fill out the following and tell us what your new life is like!

I am:
- ☐ single
- ☐ married

I live in:
- ☐ the same place I live now
- ☐ a condo in Hawaii
- ☐ a penthouse in New York City
- ☐ a beach home in California
- ☐ a house in the country with plenty of land
- ☐ a cozy chalet in the mountains of Colorado

Professionally I am:
- ☐ doing what I am doing now
- ☐ advancing in my profession
- ☐ exploring a new profession, namely _____
- ☐ happily retired
- ☐ owner of my own business
- ☐ other: _____

The most exciting thing happening in my life is:

INTRODUCTION

Step Two: TOMORROW. "Tomorrow" is a word that can be both full of hope and full of dread. It is full of hope when it brings to mind the promise of a new day for the world we live in, as well as for us personally. It is full of dread when it brings to mind uncertainty and the loss of treasured things and relationships we presently have. What "tomorrow" means for us is a choice. It is full of dread when we choose to keep our eyes focused on the past, and defensively hold on to what we have. It is full of hope when we plan for an exciting future, realizing that God has much more in store for us than we could imagine.

Sometimes when we look to the future, singles think only of the possibility of marriage. While many singles do eventually marry (and marriage can bring blessings to life), that should by no means be the main issue that we focus on. For one, it ignores the positive aspects of being single, which we considered in a previous session. But such an approach also puts things in the wrong priority. Author Sam Keen (in his book *Fire in the Belly*) writes of a mentor who told him that there are two main questions we must ask: (1) "Where am I going?" and (2) "Who will go with me?" The mentor warned him, "If you ever get these questions in the wrong order you are in trouble." This advice was originally given specifically to men, but it is true for both men and women. We first must determine where we are going in life, where God is calling us. That is the question of "vocation." The question of who will go with us— whether that be a spouse or a group of other single friends who share the road with us—is subservient to the first issue.

LEADER: Choose the Track One Bible study (below) or the Track Two study (page 60).

Looking to tomorrow (and where we are going in life) requires a willingness to leave today behind. People (and things) we have relied on in the past may not be there for us in the future. The disciples found that out. In our Track One study (from John's Gospel), we will look at how Jesus prepared them for the time when he would leave them. They would face their tomorrow without Jesus' physical presence. What he told them will also speak to us. In our Track Two study (from Paul's letter to the Philippians), we will examine personal flexibility that helps us adapt to a changing future.

BIBLE STUDY / 25 Minutes / Groups of 4

Leader: For this final session, again divide into groups of 4 (if there are more than 7 in your group). Help the groups choose their Bible study. Remind the Conveners to end their Bible study time 5 minutes earlier than usual to allow ample time for your final Caring Time—deciding what the group will do next.

Stay Tuned
John 16:5–13

STUDY | Read John 16:5–13 and discuss your responses to the following questions with your group. This passage is from a final talk Jesus had with his followers before facing his death on the cross. Referring to the notes on pages 63–64 will help you with difficult words and phrases.

⁵ *"Now I am going to him who sent me, yet none of you asks me, 'Where are you going?'* ⁶ *Because I have said these things, you are filled with grief.* ⁷ *But I tell you the truth: It is for your good that I am going away. Unless I go away, the Counselor will not come to you; but if I go, I will send him to you.* ⁸ *When he comes, he will convict the world of guilt in regard to sin and righteousness and judgment:* ⁹ *in regard to sin, because men do not believe in me;* ¹⁰ *in regard to righteousness, because I am going to the Father, where you can see me no longer;* ¹¹ *and in regard to judgment, because the prince of this world now stands condemned.*

¹² *"I have much more to say to you, more than you can now bear.* ¹³ *But when he, the Spirit of truth, comes, he will guide you into all truth. He will not speak on his own; he will speak only what he hears, and he will tell you what is yet to come."*

John 16:5–13, NIV

1. Which of the following words best describes the picture of Jesus you get from this passage?
   - ❑ mystical
   - ❑ parental
   - ❑ self-sacrificing
   - ❑ confident
   - ❑ obscure
   - ❑ protective
   - ❑ visionary
   - ❑ loving

2. Why didn't the disciples ask where Jesus was going?
   - ❑ they were afraid to
   - ❑ they already knew
   - ❑ they were angry that he was leaving and didn't want to talk about it
   - ❑ they were too busy wondering where they were going

3. What did Jesus mean when he said, "It is for your own good that I am going away"?
   - ❑ he didn't think he was doing them any good while he was alive
   - ❑ they were becoming too dependent on him
   - ❑ he had to die to bring them forgiveness
   - ❑ they had to let go of their past with him to make way for their future with the Spirit

4. When have you had a hard time letting go of something good, as the disciples did when Jesus left them?
   - ❑ when I graduated from high school and left my old friends
   - ❑ when I left the security of home
   - ❑ when I left a low-paying but enjoyable job for a higher-paying one
   - ❑ when I moved to a new town
   - ❑ other: _____

5. Who have you become so dependent on that you couldn't really grow until they were to some extent out of the picture?
   - ❑ my mom
   - ❑ a mentor
   - ❑ my former spouse
   - ❑ a counselor
   - ❑ no one
   - ❑ my dad
   - ❑ a best friend
   - ❑ a boyfriend/girlfriend
   - ❑ a pastor or teacher
   - ❑ other: _____

"The loneliest place in the world is the human heart when love is absent."
—Anonymous

6. What would you like to ask of the Spirit about "what is yet to come" (v. 13)?
   ❑ what will happen to me professionally
   ❑ what will happen to me maritally
   ❑ what will happen to me in regard to relationships
   ❑ what will happen to me in my health
   ❑ what will happen to me spiritually

7. If instead of asking Jesus, "Where are you going?" someone asked you that question, how would you answer?

8. What do you need most in order to clarify your future direction?
   ❑ freedom from past failures
   ❑ a better awareness of my strengths
   ❑ a closer relationship with the Spirit
   ❑ courage to break with the past
   ❑ courage to break from an unhealthy relationship
   ❑ training or schooling to help me expand my options

LEADER: When you have completed the Bible study, move on to the Caring Time (pages 62–63).

Stay Loose
Philippians 4:10–13

STUDY Read Philippians 4:10–13. This passage is from a letter which Paul wrote from a Roman jail. At this point, he really did not know if he had much of a future in this life. But he knew that God always gave him the flexibility to "stay loose" and meet each circumstance as it came. Discuss with your group your responses to the questions which follow this passage. If you run across a difficult word or phrase, check the Reference Notes on page 64.

> *¹⁰ I rejoice greatly in the Lord that at last you have renewed your concern for me. Indeed, you have been concerned, but you had no opportunity to show it. ¹¹ I am not saying this because I am in need, for I have learned to be content whatever the circumstances. ¹² I know what it is to be in need, and I know what it is to have plenty. I have learned the secret of being content in any and every situation, whether well fed or hungry, whether living in plenty or in want. ¹³ I can do everything through him who gives me strength.*

> *Philippians 4:10–13, NIV*

1. How would you describe Paul's attitude in this passage?
   ❑ overconfident   ❑ at peace
   ❑ positive   ❑ stoic
   ❑ empowered   ❑ flexible
   ❑ invulnerable   ❑ thankful
   ❑ independent   ❑ egotistical

"The future is an
opportunity yet
unmet, a path yet
untraveled, a life
yet unlived. But
how the future will
be lived, what
opportunities will
be met, what paths
traveled, depends
on the priorities
and purposes of
life today."
—C. Neil Strait

**LEADER: When you
have completed the
Bible study, move on
to the Caring Time
(pages 62–63).**

2. Why did Paul make a point of denying he was in need?
   - ❏ he was too proud to admit need
   - ❏ he didn't want the readers to feel obligated to help more
   - ❏ he wanted the readers to learn about his source of contentment
   - ❏ people had helped so much he really wasn't in need
   - ❏ God was supplying all of his needs

3. Which of the following would you say can be implied from Paul's teaching, "I can do everything through him who gives me strength"?
   - ❏ God will always help us to succeed
   - ❏ we need never fear the future
   - ❏ achievement is less a matter of ability than of dependence on God
   - ❏ there are no tragic circumstances; only a tragic shortage of faith
   - ❏ self-doubt is inappropriate for the believer who depends on God

4. When was a time of great plenty in your life? When was a time of great need?

5. How would you define the difference between contentment and complacency?

6. If they were a part of your future, which of these circumstances would you have trouble being content in?
   - ❏ financial failure
   - ❏ mental impairment (like Alzheimer's)
   - ❏ the death of my best friend
   - ❏ a bitter family conflict
   - ❏ a physical disability
   - ❏ the death of a son or daughter
   - ❏ having a disease (like cancer)
   - ❏ marriage and then divorce
   - ❏ other: _____

7. How confident are you that you will be able to find contentment in your tomorrow?

1	2	3	4	5	6	7	8	9	10
Not at all confident				Somewhat confident					Certain!

8. Which challenge do you think you'll need the strength that Paul talks about in verse 13?
   - ❏ facing a lifetime of being single
   - ❏ facing my own physical deterioration over time
   - ❏ achieving the things I feel driven to achieve
   - ❏ raising kids as a single parent
   - ❏ facing sexual pressures
   - ❏ dealing with my spiritual weakness
   - ❏ other: _____

CARING TIME / 25 Minutes / All Together

Leader: This is decision time. These four steps are designed to help you evaluate your group experience and to decide about the future.

EVALUATION

Take a few minutes to look back over your experience and reflect. Go around on each point and finish the sentences.

1. As you think about "tomorrow" and the challenges you will face, what role, if any, do you see for a group like this?

2. What key lessons have you learned about singleness from this series of Bible studies?

3. As I see it, our purpose and goal as a group was to:

4. We achieved our goal(s):
   - ❏ completely
   - ❏ almost completely
   - ❏ somewhat
   - ❏ we blew it

5. The high point in this course for me has been:
   - ❏ the Scripture exercises
   - ❏ the sharing
   - ❏ discovering myself
   - ❏ belonging to a real community of love
   - ❏ finding new life and purpose for my life
   - ❏ the fun of the fellowship

6. One of the most significant things I learned was...

7. In my opinion, our group functioned:
   - ❏ smoothly, and we grew
   - ❏ pretty well, but we didn't grow
   - ❏ it was tough, but we grew
   - ❏ it was tough, and we didn't grow

8. The thing I appreciate most about the group as a whole is:

CONTINUATION

Do you want to continue as a group? If so, what do you need to improve? Finish the sentence:

"If I were to suggest one thing we could work on as a group, it would be..."

MAKE A COVENANT

A covenant is a promise made to each other in the presence of God. Its purpose is to indicate your intention to make yourselves available to one another for the fulfillment of the purposes you share. In a spirit of prayer, work your way through the following sentences, trying to reach an agreement on each statement pertaining to your ongoing life together. Write out your covenant like a contract, stating your purpose, goals, and the ground rules for your group. Then ask everyone to sign.

1. The purpose of our group will be.... (finish the sentence)

2. Our goals will be...

3. We will meet for _____ weeks, after which we will decide if we wish to continue as a group.

4. We will meet from _____ to _____ and we will strive to start on time and end on time.

5. We will meet at _____ (place) or we will rotate from house to house.

6. We will agree to the following ground rules for our group (check):

   ❐ **Priority**: While you are in the course, you give the group meetings priority.

   ❐ **Participation**: Everyone participates and no one dominates.

   ❐ **Respect**: Everyone is given the right to their own opinion, and "dumb questions" are encouraged and respected.

   ❐ **Confidentiality**: Anything that is said in the meeting is never repeated outside the meeting.

   ❐ **Empty Chair**: The group stays open to new people at every meeting, as long as they understand the ground rules.

   ❐ **Support**: Permission is given to call upon each other in time of need at any time.

   ❐ **Accountability**: We agree to let the members of the group hold us accountable to the commitments which each of us make in whatever loving ways we decide upon.

CURRICULUM

If you decide to continue as a group for a few more weeks, what are you going to use for study and discipline? There are 15 other studies available at this 201 Series level. 301 Courses are for deeper Bible study also with Study Notes.

For more information about small group resources and possible direction, please contact your small group coordinator or SERENDIPITY at 1-800-525-9563.

**REFERENCE NOTES:
JOHN 16:5–13**

v. 5   **None of you asks...** Peter *did* ask this question (13:36). Jesus is responding to the fact that Peter and the others did not really understand the significance of the answer he gave to Peter's question.

v. 7   **It is for your good that I am going away...** This is what Caiaphas said, but with an entirely different intent (11:50)! Jesus' departure means the coming of the Counselor (see 14:16), which really means his return to them in a deep, inner, spiritual way (7:39; 14:15–20).

vv. 8–11 .**he will convict the world of guilt in regard to sin and righteousness and judgment**... The "world" held that Jesus was an unrighteous sinner under the judgment of God (9:24). The Spirit will prove the world wrong about its convictions on these matters. The ultimate *sin* is to reject Jesus (Ac. 2:23; 3:13–15), since he is from God and did the works of God. *Righteousness* ("justice") is shown by the Father's vindication of Jesus through his resurrection and ascension. Whereas the leaders thought Jesus was a blasphemer, the Father will exalt him. *Judgment* is the condemnation brought upon Satan as a result of Jesus' triumph over him (12:31).

v. 13 **all truth**... See 14:26. This is truth about the message of Jesus and its application to life. **He will not speak on his own**... The interrelationship of the Father, Son, and Spirit is repeated. Each member of the Trinity seeks the glory and honor of the other (see 8:54; 12:28; 16:14; 17:1, 4). **he will tell you what is yet to come**... This does not refer to fortune-telling, but to an increased understanding about who Jesus is.

Summary... While Paul affirmed the right of an apostle to be supported by the church, he personally preferred to underwrite his own ministry by working as a tentmaker (Ac. 18:3; 1 Th. 2:5–12; 2 Th. 3:7–12). This way, no one could ever accuse him of preaching the gospel in order to make money or say that the gospel was anything but a free gift (1 Cor. 9:7–18). He wants to thank them while at the same time he asks them not to send any more money.

v. 10 **that. . . you have been concerned**... The cause of his rejoicing is not the gift *per se*, but the concern that it reflected. **at last**... Apparently the Philippians had not been in contact with Paul for quite some time. However, the arrival of Epaphroditus renewed their contact with Paul (for which he is grateful). Paul is not criticizing them for not being in touch. He recognizes they simply had no opportunity.

v. 11 Having expressed his pleasure at this sign of their care, he then goes on to say: "But, in fact, I really did not need what you gave me!" This is the first of several alternations between commending them for their gift (vv. 10, 14–16, 18–20) and insisting on his right to self-sufficiency (vv. 11–13, 17). **need**... Paul was not in difficult straits financially. He accepts their gift only because it is of great benefit *to them* to give in this way (see vv. 17–18). **content**... Paul borrows this word from the vocabulary of the Stoic philosophers (who used it to describe the person who was self-sufficient and able to exist without anything or anyone). However, Paul's sufficiency is found in the Lord.

v. 12 Paul contrasts two extremes: deprivation and riches. **need**... This refers to the fundamental needs which are basic to life (such as food and water). Paul has learned to exist even in the midst of poverty. **plenty**... Lit. "to overflow." This is to have enough for one's own needs plus something left over. **I have learned**... This verb is drawn from the mystery religions and refers to the rites by which a new member comes to understand the secret of the cult. **well fed**... This word describes force-fed animals who are stuffed to overflowing, in order to fatten them for slaughter.

v. 13 **everything**... Lit. "all these things." Paul is referring to what he has just described: his ability to exist in material circumstances—wealth or poverty, abundant food or no food, etc. He is not suddenly making a general statement about his ability to do anything. **through him who gives me strength**... The "secret" Paul has learned (which enables him to live with contentment in all circumstances) is his union with Christ.

**REFERENCE NOTES:
PHILIPPIANS
4:10–13**

64